La Varenne's
PARIS KITCHEN

La Varenne's
PARIS KITCHEN

By Anne Willan

WILLIAM MORROW AND COMPANY, INC.
New York   1981

Library of Congress Cataloging in Publication Data

Willan, Anne.
    La Varenne's Paris kitchen.

    Includes indexes.
    1. Cookery, French—Study and teaching—France.
2. École de cuisine La Varenne.   3. Cookery, French.
I. Title.
TX719.W57   641.5944   80-27346
ISBN 0-688-00411-3

Printed in the United States of America

Book Design by Sallie Baldwin, Antler & Baldwin, Inc.

Acknowledgments

Three La Varenne associates have made enormous contributions to the writing of this book: The recipes were drafted and tested under the direction of Faye Levy; Judith Hill wrote the chefs' portraits and edited the manuscript; and Steven Raichlen contributed his personal word picture, "This Is La Varenne."

I am also deeply grateful to photographer James Scherer and to Morrow editor Narcisse Chamberlain.

Editorial office

Contents

*Chef Fernand Chambrette, Director of Cuisine at La Varenne,
and Anne Willan, founder and President, in the demonstration kitchen*

Foreword

I am both happy and proud to introduce my six colleagues at L'École de Cuisine La Varenne who have made such a contribution to the success of the school since it opened in 1975. The seven of us who cook at the school in Paris, and on tour in the United States, have each selected recipes that are personal favorites—dishes firmly attached to our names in the school's repertory: "Chambrette's Salmon Scallops," or "Gregory's Lamb Ragoût," or "Jorant's Brioches." La Varenne, of course, is much more than just its teachers and their recipes, so the book opens with a portrait in words and pictures of a day at the school and of the chefs, staff, trainees, and students who are the heart and soul of our *école de cuisine*.

Our recipe selections have been made with practical cooking in mind. La Varenne has a disciplined curriculum that extends to a high professional level, and it also teaches authentic French cuisine to beginners. But to be useful to all of you who will cook from this book, we have left out the simpler standard recipes that you can find elsewhere. At the same time, we have tried to avoid technically demanding recipes that are best learned on the spot in a practical class or at a demonstration. We couldn't resist including some quite magnificent creations, but in the main, we mean this introduction to La Varenne to intrigue and teach—not to stun you with the highest reaches of the French chef's art.

Director of Cuisine Chef Fernand Chambrette is famous for his preparation of fish, but his choice of recipes runs the gamut of regional dishes like Chicken en Cocotte Vallée d'Auge, through the classics, and on to the surprises of *nouvelle cuisine*. The preferences of his colleague Chef Claude Vauguet are more youthful—he blends new ideas with his classical training to fit modern tastes. *Pâtissier* Albert Jorant, third chef of the resident La Varenne trio, is outstanding for his beautifully decorated cakes and tiny, perfect *petits fours*, while Maurice Ferré, pastry chef at Maxim's, specializes in sherbets, candies, and chocolate work. The tastes of Chef Léon Zelechowski, junior member of the French team, run to healthy, low-calorie dishes, though he does break out now and then with the butter and cream. The recipes chosen by Gregory Usher and me, French cooks by adoption, are less ambitious. Our theme is unmistakably French, but we favor a simple approach. You'll find fewer ingredients in our recipes and more dishes that can be prepared ahead.

The basic recipes at the end of the book are given to every student who comes to La Varenne. These are the building blocks of French cuisine—the stocks, sauces, the pastry doughs and the creams with which so many dishes are constructed. Simple recipes like Chef Vauguet's Pork Chops Dijonnaise may call for only one basic preparation, but more complex dishes, particularly pastries and desserts, can use four or more. For example, Chef Ferré's Orange Chanteclaire is a lovely confection with five elements that are each of them recipes in their own right.

Recipes can explain the facts, but memorable cooking has something more: a balance and a sureness of touch that lifts it from the pedestrian to the brilliant. It is this harmony, based on a thorough understanding of techniques, lightened by the personal twist, that we try to teach at La Varenne and that we invite you to share in our *Paris Kitchen*.

ANNE WILLAN
August 1980

La Varenne
34, rue St. Dominique
75007 Paris

La Varenne's
PARIS KITCHEN

Students waiting in front of the school for the afternoon demonstration

This Is LaVarenne

THE WOMAN in the red-and-white striped apron has never seen a plucked duck with its head and feet still intact before, but she is determined to gut and clean this bird the way the chef showed her earlier. Her partner, a caterer from Cleveland, is performing a task the French call *peler à vif*, "skinning alive," which in this instance consists of paring the pith and membrane from oranges to leave only the juicy fruit that will garnish the duck.

The third member of their team, a burly graduate from The Culinary Institute of America, rummages among the gleaming pots and pans clustered around the large wooden post next to the worktable, looking for a *poêlon à sucre*—a copper sugar pot in which he will cook the caramel for the *sauce bigarade* that accompanies the duckling.

The three of them have traveled a combined 13,000 miles for the instruction they are receiving this morning, and the work involved in preparing their *canard à l'orange*, however taxing, could not delight them more. Each wants to learn cooking the French way and to do so has come here to La Varenne.

❀   ❀   ❀   ❀   ❀

L'École de Cuisine La Varenne is the only fully bilingual French cooking school. It is named for the father of modern French cooking, the 17th-century cook François Pierre de la Varenne. Located in the heart of Paris on the Left Bank, the school was founded five years ago

by Anne Willan to bridge the gap between the French and American food worlds.

To assure the authenticity of La Varenne's program, Anne Willan hired French-born, French-trained chefs to do the teaching. She insisted that they use French recipes, French cooking equipment, French cooking techniques, and the best available French ingredients. She decided to have full-time translators to provide dependable com-

A student assistant translates in the demonstration kitchen as Chef Fernand Chambrette cleans a chicken. Students can see everything clearly in the overhead mirrors.

munication between the chefs and the students. The classes, Anne was convinced, could be professional in their approach to cooking and teach methods that are practical in an American home kitchen as well. She planned the curriculum to offer a thorough grounding in classic French cooking, yet to be flexible enough to keep pace with the latest trends in *nouvelle cuisine*. Finally, she wanted the school to be serious, as the French are about their cooking, but also to encourage the warmth and enjoyment that, after all, says Anne, are what cooking is all about.

For Anne, the key to understanding French cooking is not the language, but the whole way the French feel and think about food. "The French are constantly discussing, analyzing, criticizing their food," she says, "and the day a child is old enough to sit at the dinner table, his participation in the gastronomic dialogue begins." Anne remembers that the first time she dined in a three-star restaurant, some twenty years ago, her host spent half an hour discussing the menu and wine list with the maître d'hôtel. "I had never known people could be so impassioned by food," she recalls with a smile. "It was an absolute revelation to me." It was then that Anne realized that to truly master the art of French cooking one has to look at, handle, and understand food as only the French do. And that the best place to acquire this French attitude and knowledge is Paris.

It took three or four years to plan and organize the school. For the site, Anne chose a 150-year-old building that had once housed a typical Parisian *bistrot*. The ground floor was remodeled to accommodate a kitchen where practical classes would take place. The second floor became the demonstration kitchen, with a three-panel mirror over the stainless-steel worktable. Adjoining rooms were soon transformed into administrative offices and the editorial department, which is charged with drafting and testing school recipes, planning menus for new courses, and researching an ever-growing number of school publications.

❂   ❂   ❂   ❂   ❂

The duck class had begun promptly at 9:30 in the morning, but La Varenne had already been buzzing with activity for hours. School Director Chef Chambrette was the first to arrive, and by 8:00 he had drunk his coffee, donned his faded blue work smock, and packed off in a minibus to go shopping at Rungis, the huge new Paris market. "To end up with good food, you must start with good ingredients," the chefs never stop telling the students. This weekly pilgrimage to

Chef Chambrette at his desk in the early morning, phoning in orders for supplies

Rungis guarantees the students the finest produce and dairy products available in France.

Chef Chambrette knows most of the merchants by name at the enormous depot, because for thirty years he handpicked the provisions destined for use at his own two-star restaurant. At each stop there are handshakes and amiable banter. During the next hour, the back of the bus fills up with impeccably fresh produce. The last to go in are a flat of ripe Provençal peaches, and another of strawberries, a crate of chicory glistening with moisture, and a small basket of rare *trompettes de la mort* mushrooms with which the chef will prepare a special ragoût. On his way back to La Varenne, Chef Chambrette speeds past the tall dome of the Invalides where Napoleon is buried, pulls the truck up on the sidewalk in front of the school, and the serious work begins.

The student assistants will not have been idle during his absence. A young Australian tidies up the *chambre froide* (the modern walk-in

17

*Chef Chambrette at Rungis,
inspecting strawberries*

A student assistant in the basement storeroom, shelling peas for the mis-en-place *of a chef's demonstration class*

refrigerator) in the basement and by the time Chambrette returns, the cold room—with meats, country hams, and poultry hanging from metal meat hooks—will be as orderly as the drawer of a cash register. Another student assistant, a former French teacher, has begun the *mise en place,* or set-up of ingredients, for the classes. She measures out each necessary comestible in the basement and then freights them all up to the first- and second-floor classrooms on the dumbwaiter. This assistant will rattle up and down the cellar stairs perhaps thirty times over the course of the day. She cannot keep from smiling each time she passes a poster tacked up on the cold-room door. It reads

In the chambre froide, *carafes
of water and wine, chickens,
rabbits, buckets of stock*

*Chef Claude Vauguet shows a student in the practical class
where to chop off the feet of a duck.*

"Women Terrorized by Chefs."

By 9:15, the first-floor kitchen begins to resemble a classroom.
Ten folding chairs have been arranged around a wooden worktable.
A *torchon*, the protean French dishtowel, which serves as a sponge,
potholder, or piece of cheesecloth, hangs over the back of each student's chair. In true restaurant-kitchen style, the ovens have been
preheated to 450°F—hot, fast, and tricky. The chef checks the ingredients and decides on his battle plan.

At 9:30, the students take their seats. *"Bonjour, messieurs et
mesdames,"* says Chef Vauguet, tipping his *toque*. As he speaks, his
assistant translates. "This morning, we will make *crème Olga, canard
à l'orange,* and *tarte feuilletée aux fruits."* For the next forty-five
minutes, the chef gives a detailed explanation of the dishes to be pre-

The first-floor practical kitchen, ready for class

pared, commenting on the ingredients, methods, and pitfalls of each recipe and demonstrating the rudimentary and the sophisticated—how to dice an onion, truss a duckling, or incorporate butter into puff pastry. The students follow the chef eagerly, but frown every time he diverges from the recipe. "Don't worry," the student assistant assures them. "It's the technique, not the recipe, that matters."

"*C'est compris?* Do you understand?" the chef asks when he has

22

finished his lecture. He divides the class into three teams and cries "À l'attaque!"

What follows during the next two and a half hours is meticulously choreographed chaos. In various corners of the compact kitchen, knives flash, pots clatter, sinks splash, oven doors squeak, voices rumble. The chef bustles from one work station to another, offering encouragement, explanation, exhortation, advice, and an occasional

*Gregory Usher, Director of
La Varenne, at his desk*

good-natured reprimand. His assistant translates the students' questions and makes sure they have the materials and cookware they need. By 11:30, the duck and puff pastry are in the oven. By 12:30, the worktables have been cleared, wiped down, and set with place mats and silverware. The chef makes a last-minute adjustment on a bunch of watercress (chefs are never satisfied) as the students line up the platters for presentation. Hot, tired, but brimming with pride, they stand back to admire the results of three hours labor.

La Varenne's Associate Director, Gregory Usher, will be dining with the class this afternoon. It is his agreeable task to inspect, discuss, and taste the meal with the students. "The success of French cooking has been a result not only of talented chefs, but of an informed and critical public," Gregory says. "In France, the connoisseur is respected just as much as the cook." The students offer their own opinions about the morning's production: the *crème Olga*—potato and mushroom soup—is pronounced delicious, but a trifle pallid. The duckling is deemed delectable to the eye as well as to the palate. The puff pastry shatters into a million buttery flakes—proof that the students have learned their lesson well. "This is the best restaurant in Paris!" exclaims Gregory, and all ten students agree.

✿   ✿   ✿   ✿   ✿

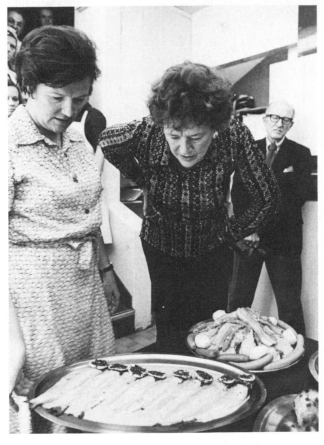

"Julia is coming to lunch!"

Mrs. Child inspects a platter of trout and a choucroute garnie just completed by students in a practical class; husband Paul watches in the background.

Sitting down to lunch with the students

After lunch, a camera session and mutual admiration: Julia and Chef Chambrette

The students lunching on duckling this afternoon are among the more than 4,000 cooking enthusiasts who have flocked to La Varenne since the school opened five years ago. Their reasons for making this culinary pilgrimage to Paris are as varied as the many cities and countries from which they come. A number of La Varenne students are restaurateurs, chefs, caterers, cooking teachers, and food writers, while others have never before held a whisk or spatula. Whether students attend La Varenne for a week-long visitors' course, or enroll in the nine-month course cycle leading to La Varenne's *grand diplôme*, they participate in the same carefully structured curriculum designed to teach the fundamentals of French cuisine. During five demonstrations each week, they will watch the chefs in the preparation of two or three delectable dishes. Four times a week, they will themselves put hand to ladle and saucepan and cook full-course menus under their instructor's watchful supervision.

Advanced students who come to the school thinking they know it all are quickly disillusioned as they watch five different chefs prepare the same pastry dough five different, perfectly "correct" ways. Students who come to La Varenne merely to collect recipes soon learn that recipes are only starting points, which the chefs constantly modify to suit the ingredients and the time available. The chefs stress the importance of classic cooking techniques and basic preparations over individual recipes. If there is one central lesson to be learned at La Varenne, it is this: Once you have mastered the building blocks of French cuisine, the creation and execution of individual dishes will follow naturally.

A student can come to La Varenne scarcely knowing how to whip cream and leave the school nine months later fully versed in the arts of making aspics and sauces, pâtés and *petits fours*, creations *en croûte* and towering *pièces montées*. In the process, he will have completed the school's orientation, intermediate, advanced, and graduate courses and seen some 1,100 recipes made in nearly 150 practical classes and over 175 demonstrations.

Short-term students join the week-long visitors' classes or choose among a variety of specialty courses covering such aspects of French cuisine as *charcuterie*, pastry, and regional cooking. The *nouvelle cuisine* course, an outgrowth of the popular weekly guest appearances, features demonstrations by talented new young chefs of the up-and-coming restaurants of Paris. From a cooking school with one full-time chef for eight students, La Varenne has become an institution and a showcase for the top culinary talent in France.

✿　　✿　　✿　　✿　　✿

The demonstration session this day covers three regional specialties from the Loire Valley: asparagus tart, sausage with pistachios and truffles, and pork cooked with a Loire wine and prunes. The chef bones a pork roast as he waits for the students to fill the demonstration room. His assistant, a young man with a master's degree in music, pits prunes that have been soaking in wine overnight. The translator taps a metal mixing bowl with a sharpening steel to signal the start of the demonstration.

The chef begins the lesson by preparing a *pâte brisée*, short pie pastry, for the asparagus tart. He sifts the flour onto the pastry marble

Staff meeting, left to right: Parke Rouse, Chairman; Anne Willan; Judith Hill and Janet Jones of the editorial staff; Chef Fernand Chambrette; Steven Raichlen; Chef Albert Jorant

in the middle of the demonstration table, makes a well in the center, and adds butter, salt, and egg yolks. "As a rule, tart pastry contains twice as much flour as butter," he tells the students as he mixes the dough. "The amount of water you add depends on the flour because old flour is 'thirstier' than fresh." He works quickly, it seems, effortlessly. Soon the finished dough is in the refrigerator being chilled. The students watch the chef's every move in the mirror overhead. He wipes the work surface and sets a cutting board on top of a folded dishtowel. "The dishtowel keeps the board from slipping," explains the assistant, as he hands the chef the tray with the ingredients for the sausages.

The preparation for the sausage began at the demonstration the day before when the meat was ground, seasoned, and set aside to absorb the flavorings. Now the chef slips a glistening pork casing over a sausage funnel and stuffs the meat into the metal tube to form the sausages. As he works he talks of *charcuterie*—the French art of making pâtés and sausages: "The *charcutier* knows that pork fat melts at 100°C, so he poaches everything at just below the boiling point. The sausages and galantines actually weigh more when they're cooked than they did raw." By now the sausages have been tied into eight-inch lengths, pricked with a carving fork, and set in a large pot to poach. The chef uses brown stock for extra flavor instead of the water called for in the recipe.

Next, the chef calls for the chilled pastry dough and deftly rolls it out to line a tart pan, discoursing on asparagus as he works. Yes, he likes the green asparagus in America, but prefers the white asparagus grown in France. No, he won't swear that asparagus is an aphrodisiac, but it's worth a try. The lined tart pan goes back into the refrigerator while he prepares the filling. The tart is assembled, with asparagus tips neatly arranged in a circle on the top. It bakes on the floor of the oven so the bottom of the crust will brown as much as the top of the filling.

Grenadins de porc aux pruneaux is the last dish slated for the afternoon, and as the chef works on the boned pork roast, he speaks of the French butcher's term for this particular cut of meat. "A *grenadin* is an inch-thick steak cut from a veal or pork loin," he says. "The same cut of lamb is called a *noisette,* 'little nut,' because it is so small." The meat is floured, sautéed, and transferred to a platter. The pan is deglazed with wine splashed cavalierly from the bottle.

"Since this dish is a specialty of the Loire Valley, a Loire wine must be used for making the sauce—we have here a white wine, a Vouvray." The class laughs as the chef pours himself a glass to taste and makes an odd face. But the translator calls the audience's attention to the way the chef tastes wine—sucking in air with the wine as it comes in contact with his palate. "The air enables you to appreciate the full flavor."

And so the demonstration goes, a mélange of cooking and commentary, until 4:30 when the three regional specialties, carefully arranged on platters, are set before the audience. Flash bulbs light up the demonstration table as students photograph the display. An assistant hands out cutlery and napkins. The chef divies up his handiwork for tasting, and the room resounds with sighs of delectation.

Demonstration classes require teamwork: One student assistant beats egg yolks and sugar, the other beats egg whites, and Chef Albert Jorant butters the mold for a sponge cake (biscuit).

As the students file out, assistants are already folding up the chairs, pushing brooms, and setting out supplies in preparation for the evening class that begins at 5:30 P.M. and will go on until 9:30.

＊　　＊　　＊　　＊　　＊

Thus concludes a day at L'École de Cuisine La Varenne for the threesome who had never before seen a plucked duck with head and feet intact. They leave the demonstration kitchen, stomachs replete, notebooks jammed with information, and their heads aswarm with ideas about food, cooking, and possibilities for the future. Already La Varenne students are making a name for themselves in the food field: Three write for *Gourmet* magazine, one cooks for the mayor of New York City, two have opened thriving cooking schools in the San Francisco Bay area, one has a TV program in Canada, and several are chefs at top restaurants. Perhaps these three aspiring cooks will join their ranks. . . .

"You cannot master the art of French cooking in a week, a month, or a year," the chefs tell the students. But each day the students learn new techniques and basic recipes; each day they grow a little more confident in procedures that just yesterday were completely new to them. This, then, is La Varenne in Paris. The spirit and expertise of its chefs pervade the recipes that follow.

Notes About the Recipes

MEASUREMENTS: Ingredient quantities are given in U.S. standard measures, with the rounded metric equivalents in parentheses.

BASIC RECIPES: These recipes, the building blocks of French cuisine, are given in detail at the back of the book and are frequently referred to in all the chef's recipes. In the lists of ingredients of the recipes, and also in the instructions, references to basic recipes are coded by a number in bold type, such as: chicken stock (**5**). The same number, again bold, and larger, appears next to the title of the corresponding basic recipe. This has been done to identify the cross-references as clearly as possible at each point where you encounter them. The basic-recipe section begins on page 205.

CRÈME FRAÎCHE: This lovely French cream is not specified in any of the recipes, as it is available only at exorbitant prices in the United States. We therefore have entered the standard American heavy cream in the lists of ingredients, because it can be used wherever the chefs normally use thick, slightly acid *crème fraîche*. In France, the counterpart of what we call heavy cream is *crème fleurette*. Practically without exception, *crème fleurette* is what is used in desserts and pastries, therefore our own heavy cream should be used for those preparations. However, in most savory recipes, *crème fraîche* is what the French would use, and unquestionably, for real French flavor and texture, it is particularly important in sauces. Making your own *crème fraîche* is no trouble at all; see *crème fraîche* (**41**) in the basic-recipe section.

The Chefs' Recipes

Fernand Chambrette

GETTING to know Chef Fernand Chambrette, the director of La Varenne, is a study in contrasts. He professes a cynical attitude toward life, yet has to bite his lower lip to keep from laughing at his own jokes. When not taking the cynic's stance, Chef Chambrette will sometimes maintain that he is a man of great simplicity and little knowledge. At others, however, he'll recommend an obscure book on the history of the French peasantry or tell you just how to test a wine to determine whether or not it has been chaptalized.

Chambrette began training for his career as a chef at the age of twelve, when he entered the École Hôtelière. At fifteen, he was ready for an apprenticeship and later became an assistant chef at Prunier, the well-known Parisian fish restaurant. After the war, in 1946, Chambrette bought the Boule d'Or, where he became famous for his fine fish dishes as well as for his terrines and game. With Chambrette as owner and chef, the restaurant was awarded two Michelin stars.

In 1975, Chef Chambrette retired from the restaurant business and came to La Varenne the following year. He teaches the perfectly prepared dishes for which his restaurant was known—*consommé Germiny, vol-au-vent aux fruits de mer, suprême de bar à l'oseille, soufflé au citron*—and also continues to invent. He finds fruit, or a chicken left in the refrigerator, or a cabbage that must be used, reflects for a few moments, and, *voilà!* . . . a new dish. Once, at the end of a recipe-testing session, he came by, picked up the bits left from the vegetable and seafood quiches that had been prepared, and came up with a tart that was better than any of those tested.

The chef is pleased with the recognition he has received for his creativity in the kitchen, but when it is suggested that he is an artist, his response is mocking. "That makes me laugh. When I started, cooking was a job. But now the chefs are movie stars. It's getting so fashionable we're going to have to develop our own Beverly Hills."

Which side of Chambrette will be on show at a given moment is anyone's guess. Studying under him is doubly fascinating, for his knowledge of cooking and his attitudes toward life are equally diverse.

Chef Fernand Chambrette,
in the practical kitchen,
chopping cabbage

Fernand Chambrette's Choices

FIRST COURSES

Cream of Cauliflower Soup, p. 38
Crab Bisque, p. 39
Stuffed Mussels Bruxelloise, p. 41
Eggs Maintenon, p. 42

MAIN COURSES

Trout Italienne, p. 44
Salmon Scallops with Spinach Mousse, p. 45
Chicken in Cocotte Vallée d'Auge, p. 47
Duck Ragoût with Pears, p. 48
Sautéed Sweetbreads with Glazed Root Vegetables, p. 49
Tournedos with Stuffed Mushrooms Ali Bab, p. 51

VEGETABLES

Carrot Purée with Mint, p. 52
Broccoli Purée, p. 53
Turnip Purée, p. 54

DESSERTS

Lemon Mousse with Caramel Sauce, p. 55
Peaches Cardinal, p. 57
Praline Soufflé Crêpes, p. 58

Cream of Cauliflower Soup
(CRÈME DUBARRY)

You will be surprised at the delicate flavor of this soup. Serve it with cheese puffs, or when time is short, small sautéed croûtons make a nice alternative.

½ medium cauliflower, divided in flowerets
salt and pepper
4 tablespoons (60 g) butter
2 medium potatoes, thinly sliced
4–5 cups (1–1.25 L) milk, white veal stock (4), or a mixture of
    both
2 tablespoons chopped chervil or parsley

For the cheese choux puffs:
choux pastry (26) made with ½ cup (65 g) flour, ½ cup (125 ml)
    water, ¼ teaspoon salt, 4 tablespoons (60 g) butter, and 2
    large eggs
¼ cup (30 g) grated Parmesan cheese

pastry bag with ⅛-inch (3 mm) plain tip

SERVES 6.

Blanch the cauliflower in boiling salted water 2 minutes and drain. In a heavy-bottomed pan melt 2 tablespoons (30 g) of the butter, add the potatoes, and press a piece of foil on top. Cover and cook gently, stirring occasionally, for 10–15 minutes or until soft. (NOTE: Do not allow them to brown; the soup should be light in color.) Add 4 cups (1 L) milk, stock (4), or a mixture of both, and the cauliflower, and salt and pepper. Cover and simmer 15–20 minutes or until vegetables are very tender. Purée the soup in a blender or food mill. Add more stock or milk if necessary; it should be creamy but not thick. Taste for seasoning and adjust if necessary. The soup can be made 2 days ahead and kept, tightly covered, in the refrigerator.

For the cheese puffs: Preheat oven to 400°F (200°C). Make the choux pastry (**26**) and beat in the grated cheese. Using the pastry bag, pipe ½-inch (1.25 cm) mounds on a baking sheet. Bake 12–15 minutes or until brown and crisp; cool on a rack. The choux can be made 1 or 2 days ahead and kept in an airtight container. The puffs will harden on standing, but since they are added to the soup, this does not matter.

To finish: Reheat the soup and stir in the chervil or parsley. Take from heat and stir in the remaining butter, piece by piece. Spoon the soup into bowls and serve the puffs separately.

Crab Bisque
(BISQUE DE CRABE)

This recipe includes the "secret" that makes many of Chambrette's recipes especially delicious—a generous addition of cream and butter at the last minute.

2 pounds (1 kg) small blue crabs
2 tablespoons oil
2 onions, finely chopped
1 garlic clove, finely chopped
2 tablespoons brandy
1 cup (250 ml) white wine
bouquet garni (**1**)
5 cups (1.25 L) white veal (**4**), chicken (**5**) or fish (**6**) stock
3 tomatoes, quartered
3 tablespoons rice
salt and pepper
pinch of saffron
pinch of cayenne pepper
3 tablespoons heavy cream

4 tablespoons (60 g) butter

For the croûtons:
3–4 slices firm, white bread, with crusts removed, diced
2 tablespoons oil and 2 tablespoons (30 g) butter (for frying)

Serves 6.

Wash the crabs and leave whole. In a large saucepan heat the oil, add the onion and garlic, and cook over low heat 3–5 minutes until they are soft but not brown. Add the crabs and sauté them over high heat, stirring occasionally, for 10–15 minutes or until they turn red. Add the brandy, wine, bouquet garni, and enough of the stock to cover the crabs. Simmer 5 minutes.

Remove the crabs from the liquid and pound them in a mortar with a pestle, or work in a blender or food processor. Return the pounded shells to the liquid and add the remaining stock, tomatoes, rice, salt and pepper. Cover and simmer 15–20 minutes or until the rice is tender. Discard the bouquet garni, purée the soup in a blender or food processor, and work it through a drum sieve or a strainer. The bisque can be prepared 24 hours ahead and kept, covered, in the refrigerator.

For the croûtons: Fry the diced bread in the oil and butter until golden brown and drain.

To finish: Bring the soup to a boil, reduce the heat, add the saffron, cayenne pepper, and cream, and simmer 2 minutes. Take the soup from the heat and stir in the butter, one small piece at a time. Taste for seasoning and adjust if necessary. Ladle into bowls and serve the croûtons separately.

Fernand Chambrette

Stuffed Mussels Bruxelloise
(MOULES FARCIES À LA BRUXELLOISE)

The mussel, pride of Brussels as well as of many French ports, is one shellfish that is plentiful and still inexpensive.

    3 quarts (3 L) large mussels
    3 tablespoons (45 g) butter
    1 onion, finely chopped
    ¼ cup (60 ml) dry white wine
    3 tablespoons oil
    2 shallots, finely chopped
    2 garlic cloves, finely chopped
    4 fresh tomatoes, peeled, seeded, and chopped
        OR 2 cups (500 ml) or 1 pound (500 g) canned tomatoes,
        drained and chopped
    pinch of thyme
    salt and pepper
    1 cup (100 g) grated Gruyère cheese
    2 tablespoons (30 g) melted butter

4–6 large, heatproof platters filled with rock salt

SERVES 4 as a main course or 6 as a first course.

Scrub the mussels thoroughly under cold running water and remove their beards. Discard any mussels that are open and do not close when tapped. In a large kettle heat 2 tablespoons (30 g) of the butter and sauté the onion until soft but not brown. Add the mussels and the white wine. Cover and cook over high heat, stirring once, for 5–7 minutes or until the shells open. Discard any mussels that do not open. Discard the top shell from each mussel and remove the rubbery ring around each. Set the mussels flat on the platters of rock salt. Reserve the liquid.

Heat the oil and the remaining 1 tablespoon (15 g) of the butter. Add the shallots, garlic, tomatoes, thyme, and salt and pepper and cook gently, stirring occasionally, until the mixture is pulpy. Add the mussel liquid (be careful not to add any sand at the bottom) and simmer 10–15 minutes or until very thick. Taste the stuffing for seasoning and adjust if necessary—the mussel liquid is often quite salty. Spoon a little over each mussel. Top with grated cheese and sprinkle with the melted butter. The mussels can be prepared to this point up to 4 hours ahead.

To finish: Broil the mussels 4–5 minutes or until very hot and lightly browned.

Eggs Maintenon
(OEUFS MOLLETS MAINTENON)

Maintenon is the name of the classic combination of mushrooms and soubise sauce enriched with egg yolks.

pie pastry (**24**) made with 2 cups (260 g) flour, ¼ pound (125 g) butter, 2 egg yolks, ¾ teaspoon salt, and 5–6 tablespoons cold water
8 eggs

For the rich soubise sauce:
soubise sauce (**15**) made with 1 cup thick béchamel sauce (**13**), 2 medium onions, 2 tablespoons (30 g) butter, salt and pepper
3 tablespoons heavy cream
3 egg yolks
3 tablespoons water

For the duxelles:
1 tablespoon (15 g) butter
1 shallot, finely chopped
10 ounces (300 g) mushrooms, finely chopped

1 tablespoon chopped parsley
salt and pepper

eight 4-inch (10 cm) tartlet pans

SERVES 8 as first course.

Make the pie pastry (**24**) and chill. Roll it out to just under ¼ inch (6 mm) thick. Arrange the buttered tartlet pans side by side, roll the dough loosely around the rolling pin, and then unroll it over the pans. Press the pastry into the pans with a ball of dough dipped in flour and roll the pin across the pans to cut off excess dough. Prick the shells with a fork and chill ½ hour or until firm. Preheat the oven to 400°F (200°C).

Line the tartlet shells with rounds of foil and fill with dried beans or rice, or place a smaller tartlet pan inside each. Put them on a baking sheet and bake in the preheated oven 8–10 minutes or until the pastry is set and lightly browned. Remove the beans and foil or small tartlet pans and return the shells to the oven 5–7 minutes or until crisp and brown. Let cool slightly, then remove from the pans, and cool completely on a rack. The shells can be made up to 48 hours ahead and kept in an airtight container.

To make the sauce: Make the soubise sauce (**15**), bring to a boil, and stir in the cream. In a small heavy-bottomed saucepan whisk the yolks with the water. Set over low heat and whisk constantly 4–5 minutes or until thickened. Whisk this mixture into the soubise sauce.

For the duxelles: In a saucepan melt the butter and slowly cook the shallot in it until soft but not brown. Add the chopped mushrooms and cook over high heat, stirring, until all the moisture has evaporated. Add the parsley with salt and pepper. Stir in 2 tablespoons of the soubise sauce.

Immerse the eggs in a saucepan of boiling water, return to a boil, and let boil 5 minutes. Refresh under cold running water until completely cold and then peel carefully.

To finish: Heat the broiler. Spoon some of the duxelles mixture into each tartlet shell. Place an egg in each, coat with the soubise sauce, and brown under the broiler.

Trout Italienne
(TRUITE À L'ITALIENNE)

A l'Italienne does not mean that this recipe is Italian, but that it makes use of typically Italian ingredients. Salmon, sea bream, red mullet, whiting, or turbot fillets can also be used in this dish instead of trout.

3 shallots, finely chopped
salt and pepper
4 large trout (about ¾ pound or 375 g each)
2 very thin slices (2½ ounces or 75 g) prosciutto or other raw
    ham
2 very thin slices (2½ ounces or 75 g) cooked ham
3 tablespoons (45 g) butter
½ pound (250 g) mushrooms, very finely chopped
2 tomatoes, peeled, seeded, and chopped
1 tablespoon tomato paste
3–4 leaves chopped fresh basil or a pinch of dry basil
3–4 tablespoons white veal stock (4) or tomato sauce (18)
¼ cup (25 g) dry bread crumbs
juice of ½ lemon

SERVES 4.

Butter an ovenproof platter generously. Sprinkle with ⅔ of the shallots and with salt and pepper. Fillet the trout, remove the skin, and put the fillets on the platter. Grind both types of ham together in a food processor or chop them into the finest pieces possible.

Melt 1 tablespoon (15 g) of the butter, add the remaining shallots, and cook slowly until soft but not brown. Add the mushrooms and a little salt and pepper and cook over high heat, stirring, until nearly all the liquid has evaporated. In another pan cook the tomatoes over high heat, stirring, about 10 minutes or again until nearly all the liquid has evaporated. Remove from the heat and add the mushroom mixture, tomato paste, ground ham, basil, and veal stock (4) or tomato sauce (**18**). Taste for seasoning and leave to cool. Spread the mixture over the fillets, completely covering them, and sprinkle with the bread crumbs. Melt the remaining 2 tablespoons (30 g) butter and drizzle on top. The fish can be prepared 2–3 hours ahead and kept, covered, in the refrigerator.

Twenty to thirty minutes before serving, preheat the oven to 450°F (230°C). Bake the trout 7–10 minutes or until it just turns opaque. If the topping is not brown, brown lightly under the broiler. Squeeze lemon juice over the trout and serve.

Salmon Scallops with Spinach Mousse
(ESCALOPES DE SAUMON À LA MOUSSE D'ÉPINARDS)

Chef Chambrette is a purist concerning salmon and disdains the frozen variety. He says he'd rather eat canned sardines. For this dish, the salmon can be replaced by another firm-fleshed fish such as turbot.

4-pound (1.75 kg) piece of salmon, with bones
fish stock (**6**) made with 1 medium onion, 1 tablespoon (15 g) butter, the fish bones, 1 quart (1 L) water, 10 peppercorns, and a bouquet garni (**1**)
4 shallots, finely chopped
½ cup (125 ml) dry white wine or vermouth
salt and pepper
1 tablespoon heavy cream
½ pound (250 g) cold butter
few drops of lemon juice

For the spinach mousse:
2 pounds (1 kg) spinach
1 tablespoon (15 g) butter
salt and pepper

pinch of grated nutmeg
2 egg whites

SERVES 6–8 as a first course or 4 as a main dish.

Fillet the salmon and remove the skin. Cut each fillet in thin diagonal slices (escalopes). Make the fish stock (6) and strain. Preheat the oven to 350°F (175°C).

Butter a sauté pan or shallow baking dish generously and sprinkle with the shallots. Place the salmon scallops on top, pour the white wine over them and enough fish stock to just cover, and sprinkle with salt and pepper. Bring to a boil on top of the stove. Cover with buttered paper and poach in the oven 2–3 minutes or until the fish is lightly cooked. Let cool slightly, then lift out the fish, and let it dry on paper towels. Strain the cooking liquid and return the salmon to the dry sauté pan.

For the spinach mousse: Remove the stems and wash the spinach leaves. Blanch in a large pan of boiling salted water 2–3 minutes or just until tender. Refresh under cold running water, squeeze out the excess moisture, and purée in a food processor. In a small saucepan heat the butter and spinach, stirring constantly, for 2–3 minutes or until most of the liquid evaporates. Season with salt and pepper and nutmeg.

Boil the salmon cooking liquid with the remaining fish stock until reduced to 2–3 tablespoons. Add the cream and reduce again. Beat in the butter gradually in small pieces. Work sometimes over very low heat and sometimes off the heat, so the butter softens and thickens the sauce without melting. Add lemon juice, salt and pepper. Keep warm on a rack over warm, not boiling, water while reheating the fish.

Cover the salmon with foil and reheat in a preheated 400°F (200°C) oven just until hot. Meanwhile, finish the spinach mousse: Whip the egg whites until stiff. Bring the spinach purée to a boil, take from the heat, and add the beaten egg whites, whisking vigorously. Return to a boil, still whisking vigorously, and remove from the heat. Taste for seasoning. Arrange the salmon on top of the spinach mousse and spoon the sauce over the fish.

Fernand Chambrette

Chicken in Cocotte Vallée d'Auge
(POULET EN COCOTTE VALLÉE D'AUGE)

The Auge Valley is in Normandy, which is famed for its cream, apples, and Calvados.

2 tablespoons (30 g) butter
3½–4 pound (1.75 kg) whole roasting chicken, trussed
18–20 baby onions, peeled
salt and pepper
½ pound (250 g) mushrooms, quartered
¼ cup (60 ml) Calvados
3 egg yolks
1 cup (250 ml) heavy cream
1 tablespoon chopped parsley

SERVES 4.

Preheat the oven to 375°F (190°C). In a deep heatproof casserole melt the butter and brown the chicken on all sides. Take it out and brown the onions. Take them out, replace the chicken, and sprinkle with salt and pepper. Cover and cook in the heated oven ¾–1 hour or until the juices run clear rather than pink when the thigh is pierced with a skewer. Add the onions 20 minutes before the end of the cooking time and the mushrooms 10 minutes before the end of cooking time.

When the chicken is done, pour the Calvados over it, bring to a boil, and flame. When the flame dies, transfer the chicken to a carving board and keep warm. Leave the vegetables in the pan, boil the cooking juices to a glaze, and let cool slightly. Mix the yolks and cream and stir them into the juices. Heat the sauce gently, stirring constantly, until it thickens. (NOTE: If it gets too hot, it will curdle.) Taste for seasoning and keep warm.

Carve the chicken, arrange it on a platter, and spoon the vegetables and sauce over it. Sprinkle with the chopped parsley and serve any remaining sauce separately.

Duck Ragoût with Pears
(RAGOÛT DE CANARD AUX POIRES)

This recipe is a recent creation by Chef Chambrette—the result of a leftover duck and some extra pears. For even more flavor, he suggests making brown stock (2) for the sauce with the back and wings of the duck.

1 small duck (4 pounds or 1.75 kg)
1 tablespoon oil
1 tablespoon (15 g) butter
salt and pepper
3 large pears
1 lemon
2 tablespoons brown sugar
¼ cup (60 ml) white-wine vinegar
¾ cup (185 ml) basic brown sauce (9)

SERVES 4.

Remove the wings of the duck. Remove the legs and cut each into 2 pieces at the joint. Cutting along the breastbone, remove the entire breast in one or two boneless pieces and trim off excess fat.

In a large sauté pan heat the oil and butter. Season the pieces of duck. Add the leg and thigh pieces to the hot fat and brown on all sides over high heat. Add the breast and brown it also. Continue cooking over low heat, turning occasionally, for 20–30 minutes or until deep brown.

Peel and quarter the pears and rub with a cut lemon. Add them to the pan, cover, and stew gently with the duck over low heat about 15 minutes. Transfer the pears to a platter—they should still be rather firm. Add the brown sugar to the stew, stir well over low heat, and add the vinegar. Bring to a boil and then simmer 10 minutes. Skim as much excess fat as possible from the liquid and add the basic brown sauce (9). Simmer 15 minutes more and taste for seasoning. Return the pears to the sauce and simmer about 5 minutes more or until the duck and pears are tender. The duck can be cooked 48 hours ahead; keep it in the sauce, covered, in the refrigerator.

To serve, reheat the duck if necessary. Slice the breast into thin strips. Arrange them on a platter or plates. Arrange the leg and thigh pieces around them and garnish with the pears. Reheat the sauce, skim off excess fat again, and spoon the sauce over the duck pieces.

Sautéed Sweetbreads with Glazed Root Vegetables
(ESCALOPES DE RIS DE VEAU POÊLÉES AUX RACINES)

This is a dish for springtime when young vegetables are available, though later vegetables "turned" to the same size for even cooking can be used.

2–3 pairs (1½ pounds or 750 g) veal sweetbreads
court bouillon (7) made with 1 quart (1 L) water, 1 carrot and
    1 onion, both sliced, a bouquet garni (1), 6 peppercorns, 1
    teaspoon salt, and ¼ cup (60 ml) lemon juice
Madeira sauce (11) made with 1 cup (250 ml) basic brown sauce
    (9) and ¼ cup (60 ml) Madeira
8 carrots
1 small celery root
4 turnips
5 ounces (150 g) butter
salt and pepper
½ teaspoon sugar
½ cup (65 g) flour
2 tablespoons oil

SERVES 4.

Soak the sweetbreads 2–3 hours in cold water, changing the water once or twice. Meanwhile, make the court bouillon (7). Drain the sweetbreads, rinse, and put them in a pan with the court bouillon. Bring slowly to a boil, skimming occasionally, and simmer 10 minutes. Drain, rinse the sweetbreads again, and skin them, also removing the ducts. Press them between two plates with a 2-pound (1 kg) weight on top and leave to cool completely.

Make the Madeira sauce (11).

Cut the carrots into 1½-inch (3.75 cm) lengths and use a sharp paring knife to trim each piece to an olive shape. Shape the celery root and turnips in similar-sized, olive-shaped pieces. In a sauté pan or shallow saucepan bring the carrots to a boil with 2 tablespoons (30 g) of the butter, salt and pepper, sugar, and water to just cover. Simmer 15–20 minutes or until nearly tender. In another pan bring the celery root to a boil with 2 tablespoons (30 g) butter, salt and pepper, and water to cover. Simmer 15–20 minutes or until nearly tender. In a third pan bring the turnips to a boil with 2 tablespoons (30 g) butter, salt and pepper, and water to cover. Simmer 5–6 minutes or until nearly tender.

Cut the sweetbreads into ½-inch-thick (1.25 cm) diagonal slices. Season and coat lightly in flour. In a large sauté pan or skillet heat the oil and 2 tablespoons (30 g) butter and sauté the sweetbreads, in 2 batches if necessary, over medium heat 8–10 minutes or until tender and golden brown on both sides. Transfer the sweetbreads to a platter or to plates and keep warm.

Reheat each of the root vegetables, boiling down the liquid until it becomes a glaze. Add the Madeira sauce to the sweetbread pan and bring to a boil, stirring. Arrange the vegetables around the sweetbreads. Remove the sauce from the heat, whisk in the last of the butter in small pieces, strain, and serve the sauce separately.

Fernand Chambrette

Tournedos with Stuffed Mushrooms Ali Bab
(TOURNEDOS ALI BAB)

Ali Bab was a well-known French gourmet of the 1920s. This recipe can be varied in many ways: The ham can be replaced by tongue, the mushrooms by truffles, the veal stock by beef stock, the port by Madeira or sherry, and the croûtons of bread by croûtons of brioche or rounds of puff pastry.

4 tournedos cut 1½–2 inches (4–5 cm) thick

For the sauce:
5 tablespoons (80 g) butter
¼ cup (30 g) flour
3 cups (750 ml) brown veal stock (**2**)
bouquet garni (**1**)
salt and pepper
⅓ cup (80 ml) port wine

For the stuffed mushrooms:
4 large mushrooms
3 ounces (90 g) chopped cooked ham or Canadian bacon
1 egg yolk
juice of ¼ lemon
pinch of pepper
salt—optional

For the croûtons:
4 slices bread
3 tablespoons oil and 3 tablespoons (45 g) butter (for frying)

SERVES 4.

For the sauce: In a saucepan melt 3 tablespoons (45 g) of the butter, add the flour, and cook, stirring, until browned. Add the brown veal stock (**2**), bouquet garni, and seasoning and bring to a boil, stirring. Simmer, uncovered, for 30–45 minutes until the sauce is well-flavored and glossy. Add the port and strain. Taste for seasoning and adjust if necessary.

For the stuffed mushrooms: Preheat the oven to 350°F (175°C).

51

Remove the mushroom stems and chop them. Mix with the chopped ham or bacon, egg yolk, lemon juice, and pepper to taste. (NOTE: If the ham is well-flavored, salt may not be needed.) Mound the mixture in the mushroom caps. Arrange the mushrooms in a buttered baking dish and bake 15–20 minutes or until tender. Both sauce and mushrooms can be prepared up to 24 hours ahead and kept, covered, in the refrigerator.

To finish: If possible, have the steaks at room temperature. For the croûtons, cut rounds the same diameter as the steaks from the bread. Reheat the mushrooms and sauce if necessary. In a heavy-bottomed frying pan heat the oil and butter and fry the croûtons, turning them to brown both sides. Drain on paper towels. Pour off all but 2 tablespoons fat and sauté the tournedos in the same pan, allowing 3–4 minutes on each side for rare steak. Season the steaks after turning them.

To finish the sauce: Take it from the heat and whisk in the remaining 2 tablespoons (30 g) butter, a small piece at a time. Keep the sauce hot, but do not allow it to boil or it will separate.

Put the tournedos on the croûtons, spoon a little sauce over them, and set a mushroom on each one. Serve the remaining sauce separately.

Carrot Purée with Mint
(PURÉE CRÉCY À LA MENTHE)

Many French dishes that include carrots are named after Crécy—a small town west of Paris that is noted for producing particularly good ones.

1½ pounds (750 g) carrots
1 tablespoon (15 g) butter
½–1 teaspoon sugar—optional
salt and pepper
¼ cup (60 ml) heavy cream
1 tablespoon chopped mint leaves

SERVES 4.

Scrape and slice the carrots. Bring to a boil in salted water to cover and cook 8–10 minutes or until very tender. Drain and purée them in a blender or food processor or work them through a food mill.

In a pan melt the butter, add the carrot purée, and heat. Add sugar, and salt and pepper and beat in the cream a little at a time. Add the mint and taste for seasoning. The purée can be made 2–3 days ahead and kept, covered, in the refrigerator.

To serve, reheat the purée if necessary. Pile in a bowl and mark the top with waves made with a knife.

Broccoli Purée
(PURÉE DE BROCOLIS)

Two or three vegetable purées of different colors make an attractive garnish for roasted, grilled, or sautéed meats. Purées are especially appealing served in boat-shaped pastry shells (see Morel Tartlets, p. 62).

1 bunch (about 2 pounds or 1 kg)broccoli
2 tablespoons (30 g) butter
pinch of grated nutmeg
salt and pepper
1–2 tablespoons heavy cream

SERVES 4.

Divide the broccoli into pieces and peel the thick outer skin from the stems so they will cook evenly. Cook in boiling salted water 7–10 minutes or until just tender. Drain very thoroughly and purée in a blender or food processor or work through a food mill. The purée can be prepared 1 day ahead and kept, covered, in the refrigerator.

To finish: Melt the butter, add the purée with the nutmeg, and salt and pepper, and cook, stirring, until very hot. Stir in the cream; the purée should be just soft enough to fall from the spoon. Taste for seasoning and adjust if necessary.

Turnip Purée

(PURÉE FRENEUSE)

Potatoes that have been chilled and reheated invariably taste stale, so do not make any purée containing them more than a couple of hours before serving.

> 4 tablespoons (60 g) butter
> 3–4 medium turnips (1 pounds or 500 g), peeled and thinly sliced
> 2 medium potatoes (½ pound or 250 g)
> 1 cup (250 ml) milk
> salt and pepper
> pinch of grated nutmeg
> 1 tablespoon heavy cream—optional

SERVES 4.

In a heavy-bottomed pan melt 3 tablespoons (45 g) of the butter, add the turnips, and cover with foil and the lid. Cook gently, stirring occasionally, for 10–15 minutes until slightly soft but not brown.

Peel the potatoes and cut into thin slices. Do not soak them in water as this removes some of their starch. Add them to the softened turnips with the milk, salt and pepper, and nutmeg. Cover and simmer 15–20 minutes or until the vegetables are very tender. Drain them and work through a food mill. (NOTE: The milk can be used for soup.) The purée can be prepared up to 2 hours ahead. Keep it warm in a water bath or covered at room temperature.

To finish: Reheat the purée if necessary and taste for seasoning. Beat in the remaining 1 tablespoon (15 g) butter and the cream. Serve as soon as possible.

Lemon Mousse with Caramel Sauce
(MOUSSE DE CITRON, SAUCE CARAMEL)

The egg, sugar, and lemon mixture for this mousse must be beaten until very thick. La Varenne chefs say that it's thick enough when you can write your name with it.

For the mousse:
¼ ounce (7 g) gelatin
½ cup (125 ml) water
2 eggs
2 egg yolks
⅓ cup (65 g) sugar
grated rind and juice of 2 lemons
1 cup (250 ml) heavy cream, lightly whipped

For the caramel sauce:
1 cup (200 g) sugar
½ cup (125 ml) cold water
½ cup (125 ml) warm water

For decoration:
Chantilly cream (36) made with 1 cup (250 ml) heavy cream,
    1 tablespoon sugar, and 1 teaspoon vanilla extract
5–6 candied violets—optional

1-quart (1 L capacity) ring or kugelhopf mold
pastry bag with medium star tip

SERVES 4.

For the mousse: Dampen the ring mold (preferably made of tin-lined copper or stainless steel). In a small pan sprinkle the gelatin over the water and let stand 5 minutes or until spongy. In a bowl combine the eggs and egg yolks and gradually beat in the sugar, grated lemon rind, and juice. Set the bowl over a pan of simmering water and beat with a whisk or rotary beater 5–8 minutes or until the mixture is light and thick enough to leave a ribbon trail when the beater is lifted. Remove the bowl from the pan of hot water and continue beating. Meanwhile, melt the gelatin over low heat, beat into the warm lemon mixture, and continue beating until cool.

Set the bowl over a pan of ice water and chill it, stirring occasionally, until the mixture starts to set. Fold in the lightly whipped cream and pour into the mold. Cover and chill at least 2 hours or until firmly set. The mousse can be kept, covered, up to 24 hours in the refrigerator.

For the caramel sauce: Heat the sugar with the cold water until the sugar dissolves, bring to a boil, and cook steadily to a rich caramel brown; it must be well browned, but do not let it burn. Take from the heat and at once add the warm water, standing back because the caramel will sputter. Heat gently to melt the caramel in the water and let cool. This caramel sauce can be prepared 24 hours ahead.

Up to 2 hours before serving, dip the bottom of the mold in hot water for a few seconds, run a small knife around the edge of the mousse to release the airlock, and unmold onto a platter. Make the Chantilly cream. With the pastry bag pipe rosettes of cream onto the mousse and a ruffle around the base. Top the rosettes with the candied violets. Keep in the refrigerator. Serve the caramel sauce separately.

Fernand Chambrette

Peaches Cardinal
(PÊCHES CARDINAL)

Variations of this classic dessert are fashionable at nouvelle-cuisine restaurants in Paris. Try fresh pears, for instance, or apricots with the same colorful sauce. Cardinal refers to the brilliant red of the raspberries.

⅔ cup (135 g) sugar
2 cups (500 ml) water
pared zest and juice of 1 lemon
vanilla bean
6–8 ripe freestone peaches

For the raspberry sauce:
1 quart (500 g) fresh raspberries
    OR 1 pound (500 g) frozen raspberries, thawed
1 tablespoon kirsch
3–4 tablespoons (25–35 g) powdered sugar, or to taste

SERVES 6.

Make a syrup by heating the sugar in the water until dissolved. Add the lemon zest and juice and the vanilla bean. Halve the peaches and immerse in the syrup. (NOTE: You may have to cook the peaches in 2 batches.) Poach 8–12 minutes or until just tender. Leave to cool in the syrup, then drain, and reserve the syrup. Peel the peaches.

For the sauce: Purée the raspberries in a blender with the kirsch and powdered sugar. If using fresh raspberries, add a little of the reserved syrup to make a sauce of coating consistency.

Put the peaches in a bowl and strain the sauce over them. Cover tightly and chill at least 2 hours and up to 8 hours, so the fruit absorbs the flavor of the sauce. Serve from a glass bowl or on individual serving dishes.

Praline-Soufflé Crêpes
(CRÊPES SOUFFLÉES PRALINÉES)

The idea of cooking a soufflé mixture inside crêpes is a purely French frivolity. The praline-soufflé mixture expands as usual so that each crêpe puffs dramatically.

crêpes (32) made with 1 cup (130 g) flour
    ¼ teaspoon salt, 1 cup (250 ml) milk, 3 eggs,
    2 tablespoons (30 g) melted butter or oil, and
    4 tablespoons (60 g) clarified butter or oil (for frying)

For the soufflé mixture:
pastry cream (34) made with 3 egg yolks,
    ½ cup (100 g) sugar, 5 tablespoons (45 g) flour, 1 cup (250 ml)
       milk, pinch of salt, and 1 vanilla bean
    OR ½ teaspoon vanilla extract
praline (39) made with ½ cup (100 g) sugar and ⅔ cup (100 g)
       whole unblanched almonds
    4 egg whites

MAKES 16–18 crêpes and serves 6–8.

Make the crêpes (32) and the pastry cream (34) and praline (39) for the soufflé mixture.

To finish: About ½ hour before serving, preheat the oven to 375°F (190°C). Beat the egg whites until very stiff. Meanwhile, heat the pastry cream until hot to the touch. Fold it and the praline into the whites as lightly as possible. Put about 2 tablespoons soufflé mixture on each crêpe, fold in half, and set on a buttered heatproof platter. Bake immediately 10–12 minutes or until puffed. Serve at once.

Claude Vauguet

THE POPULAR image of a French chef as a temperamental artist is belied by Claude Vauguet—a man of imperturbable good humor. Under his tutelage, La Varenne students painstakingly reduce onions, carrots, and mounds of mushrooms to the required fine, uniform dice. The chef himself chops with mechanical speed and regularity, the blade unwavering as he casually looks up to make a comment or a joke. He teases Americans about being too gadget-minded in the kitchen (dark-eyed Chef Vauguet is French to the core), but when he turns from chopping to the next task, he may pick up a native implement, grin, and say, "In France, it's not a gadget; it's a necessary tool." Claude's special province is meats which, in the proper fashion, he tests for doneness with his fingers. A pinch with thumb and forefinger tells him whether a ragoût is almost ready or perfectly tender; a poke informs him whether a fillet of beef is rare or medium rare.

Such abilities must be developed. Chef Vauguet began his apprenticeship at fourteen, working twelve-hour days at a restaurant in the Loire, a region famous for fruits, delicious fish, and its delicate *sauce beurre blanc*. At seventeen, he came to Paris to work under the illustrious and demanding two-star chef Fernand Chambrette. In addition to moving up through the ranks to become Chef Chambrette's top assistant, Claude has catered parties, cooked for an officer's mess in Algeria during his military service, and worked as a *maître d'hôtel*. He is also bringing up two sons; the elder is now in his teens and starting his own apprenticeship with a top Paris *pâtissier*.

59

Claude has been with La Varenne since 1977 and says, "I work harder here than I would in a restaurant because our repertoire is so broad; part of the fun is that no two days of the year are the same. Who has ever heard of a restaurant with one thousand five hundred recipes?"

Chef Claude Vauguet working on a fish fillet in a demonstration

Claude Vauguet's Choices

Morel Tartlets

(BARQUETTES AUX MORILLES)

Despite his traditional training, Chef Claude is not against machines. He often makes the pastry dough for this recipe in a food processor. The mushroom mixture can be served without the pastry boats as an accompaniment to chicken or veal.

½ pound (250 g) fresh morels OR 2 ounces (60 g) dried morels
3 tablespoons (45 g) butter
1 onion, finely chopped
salt and pepper
pinch of grated nutmeg
2 tablespoons (15 g) flour
1¼ cups (310 ml) heavy cream
pie pastry (**24**) made with 1½ cups (195 g) flour, 6 tablespoons (95 g) unsalted butter, 1 egg yolk, ½ teaspoon salt, and 4–5 tablespoons cold water
1 tablespoon chopped parsley

Twenty 2½-inch (6 cm) barquette molds

MAKES about 20 boat-shaped tartlets.

If using dried morels, soak 3–4 hours in cold water to cover, drain, and chop. If using fresh morels, wash in several changes of water, brushing to remove all the sand, and chop. In a sauté pan melt the butter and cook the onion slowly until soft but not brown. Add the morels, salt and pepper, and nutmeg and cook briskly, stirring, 4–5 minutes or until tender. (NOTE: If cooked too slowly, the morels will be mushy.) Stir in the flour, cook 1 minute, then add the cream. Bring to a boil, stirring, taste for seasoning, and simmer 5–6 minutes. The morels can be prepared up to 2 days ahead and kept, covered, in the refrigerator.

Make the pie pastry (**24**) and chill 30 minutes. Preheat the oven to 400°F (200°C). Roll out the dough to just under ¼ inch (6 mm) thick. Arrange the molds close together near the dough. Wrap the dough loosely around the rolling pin and then unroll it over the molds. Press the pastry into the molds with a small piece of dough dipped in flour and roll the rolling pin across the molds to cut off the excess dough. Prick the shells, line the molds with pieces of foil, and fill with dried beans. Alternatively, put a smaller, buttered boat-shaped mold inside each one. Bake about 8 minutes or until lightly browned. Remove beans and foil or smaller molds and continue baking the shells 3–4 minutes. They may be made ahead and stored for 48 hours in an airtight container.

Just before serving, heat the boats in a preheated low oven. Reheat the morels and spoon into the heated shells. Sprinkle with the parsley and serve immediately.

Terrine of Duck with Orange
(TERRINE DE CANARD À L'ORANGE)

This terrine should be just delicately flavored with orange to allow the flavor of the duck to predominate.

1 pound (500 g) bacon, rind removed and thinly sliced, or barding fat
5–5½-pound (2.5–2.75 kg) duck
3 tablespoons Grand Marnier
2 tablespoons brandy
salt and pepper
1 pound (500 g) pork, half fat and half lean
2 chicken livers and the duck liver
1 medium onion, quartered
½ teaspoon ground allspice
2 eggs
grated zest of 2 oranges
4 slices seedless navel orange

To seal the terrine:
⅓ cup (45 g) flour
2–3 tablespoons water

2-quart (2 L) terrine with tight-fitting lid

SERVES 10.

Cover the bottom and sides of the terrine with overlapping bacon strips or barding fat. Reserve a few strips for the top.

Remove the duck skin and discard or, if it is not too fatty, use it as additional lining for the terrine. Cut breast meat into large strips and marinate in Grand Marnier, brandy, and salt and pepper for 1 hour. Cut away all other meat from the duck, discarding excess fat, and grind it with the pork, livers, and onion. Add the allspice, eggs, and orange zest and the marinade drained from the duck breast. Add plenty of salt and pepper. Sauté a teaspoon of the mixture to taste it for seasoning. Preheat the oven to 350°F (175°C).

Pack the terrine with alternating layers of the ground-meat mixture and the duck strips, beginning and ending with the ground meat. Top with the remaining bacon strips and cover with the terrine lid.

To seal the terrine: Mix the flour and water to make a heavy paste and use this to seal the gap between the lid and the mold.

Set the terrine in a water bath and bring to a boil. Cook, in the water bath, in the preheated oven 1¼–1½ hours or until a skewer inserted in the terrine through the hole of the lid for 30 seconds is hot to the touch when withdrawn. Cool to tepid. Uncover, set a plate inside the terrine rim with a 2-pound (1 kg) weight on top, and chill. The terrine should be kept at least 2 days or up to 1 week in the refrigerator so the flavor mellows.

To finish: Remove the bacon slices from the top and scrape off any fat. The terrine can be served from the mold or turned out onto a platter. Arrange the orange slices down the center.

Claude Vauguet

Provençal Scallops
(COQUILLES ST. JACQUES À LA PROVENÇALE)

Garlic is the predominant flavor of this dish, hence the name Provençal. However, the amount can be adjusted to taste. Be sure to cook the scallops only briefly or else they will toughen.

1 lemon
2 garlic cloves, finely chopped
2 shallots, finely chopped
2 tablespoons chopped parsley
1½ pounds (750 g) scallops
¼ cup (30 g) flour, seasoned with salt and pepper
2 tablespoons oil and 2 tablespoons (30 g) butter (for sautéing)

SERVES 6–8 as a first course or 4 as a main course.

With a sharp or serrated knife cut the peel from the lemon. Cut the segments away from the inner white skin, then cut the flesh into small dice. Mix with the garlic, shallots, and parsley.

Cut off and discard the small membrane, if it is still there, at the side of each scallop. Toss the scallops in the seasoned flour until coated. In a frying pan, heat the oil and butter, add the scallops, and cook over high heat until browned, allowing 2–3 minutes on each side. (NOTE: The scallops should not be crowded in the pan; cook in 2 batches if necessary. For small bay scallops, the cooking time may be only 2–3 minutes in all.) Remove and keep warm. Add the lemon mixture to the pan, sauté 1–2 minutes, and pour over the scallops. Pile in scallop shells or on plates and serve at once.

Shellfish Quiche
(QUICHE AUX FRUITS DE MER)

This recipe calls for various raw shellfish, which give an outstanding, fresh flavor. However if none are available, you can substitute cooked lobster or crab meat.

pie pastry (**24**) made with 1 cup (130 g) flour, 4 tablespoons (60 g) unsalted butter, 1 egg yolk, ¼ teaspoon salt, and 3–4 tablespoons cold water
¾ pound (350 g) raw scampi, in shells
1 quart (1 L) fresh mussels
⅓ pound (150 g) raw scallops
salt and pepper

For the custard:
2 eggs
¼ cup (60 ml) milk
¾ cup (185 ml) heavy cream
salt and pepper
pinch of grated nutmeg

shallow 7–8-inch (18–20 cm) tart or pie pan

SERVES 4.

Make the pie pastry (**24**) and chill 30 minutes.

Preheat the oven to 400°F (200°C). Lightly butter the tart pan. Roll out the dough, line the pan with it, and chill until firm. Prick the shell with a fork. Line the dough with foil, pressing it well into the base, fill with dried beans or rice, and bake 10–12 minutes until the pastry is set and beginning to brown. Remove the beans and foil and bake the shell 8–10 minutes more or until lightly browned. Remove from the oven and let the shell cool slightly. Lower the oven temperature to 375°F (190°C).

Wash the mussels thoroughly and remove the beards. Discard any open shells that do not close when tapped. Put in a saucepan over high heat and cover. Toss occasionally until just open, about 5 minutes. Shell the mussels and remove the string-like part surrounding each one. Shell the raw scampi and cut each into 4–5 pieces. Cut each scallop horizontally into 2–3 slices, discarding the small membrane on the side of each. Arrange the scallops, scampi, and mussels in the pie shell and season lightly.

For the custard: Beat together the eggs, milk, and cream until smooth; season well with salt and pepper and nutmeg.

Pour enough of the custard into the pie shell to fill it three quarters full. Bake the quiche in the preheated oven 15 minutes or until partly set. Then add more custard to completely fill the shell and bake another 15 minutes or until set and browned. (NOTE: Do not overcook or the custard will curdle.) Serve hot or cool, but not chilled. The quiche is best eaten the day it is baked.

Crown of Turbot with Red Peppers
(COURONNE DE TURBOT AUX POIVRONS)

The key to this dish is sweet red peppers, which decorate the "crown" of turbot fillets. The turbot is presented in two ways at once—as fillets that enclose a rich turbot mousseline. Flounder or whiting can replace turbot in the mousseline, and salmon is a colorful substitute for the fillets.

8 turbot fillets (about 1½ pounds or 750 g)
1 red bell pepper, seeded and cut into ¼-inch (6 mm) strips
white butter sauce (22) made with 3 tablespoons white-wine
  vinegar, 3 tablespoons dry white wine, 2 finely chopped
  shallots, ½ pound (250 g) cold butter, salt and white pepper

For the filling:
1 pound (500 g) turbot fillets
5 tablespoons (80 g) butter, softened
2 egg yolks
salt and pepper

pinch of grated nutmeg
pinch of cayenne pepper
1 egg white
⅔ cup (160 ml) heavy cream

1-quart (1 L) ring mold

SERVES 6.

For the filling: Purée the 1 pound (500 g) of fillets in a food processor. Add the butter and egg yolks and continue to process. Alternatively, work the fish twice through the fine blade of a grinder and then work in the butter and yolks in a blender. If possible, also work the mixture through a fine drum sieve. Put the purée into a metal bowl set in a pan of ice water. Add salt and pepper, nutmeg, and cayenne pepper. With a wooden spoon beat in the egg white. Gradually beat in the cream, taste for seasoning, and adjust if necessary.

Blanch the red-pepper strips in boiling water 2 minutes. Rinse in cold running water and drain.

Preheat the oven to 350°F (175°C) and butter the mold. With the side of a heavy knife or cleaver pound the fillets between two pieces of waxed paper, then cut the fillets into wide, diagonal strips. Line the mold, alternating the fillets with the red-pepper strips. Leave the ends of the fillets hanging over the edge of the mold. Spoon the filling into the mold, fold the fillet ends over it, and cover the mold with buttered foil. The mold can be assembled 3–4 hours ahead and cooked just before serving.

To finish: Set the mold in a water bath and bring to a boil on top of the stove. Put in the preheated oven and cook 30–35 minutes or until firm to the touch. Leave in a warm place 10 minutes. Meanwhile, make the white butter sauce (**22**). Tip the mold sideways to drain off any excess liquid. Unmold the crown of fish onto a heated platter and wipe away any liquid with paper towels. Coat the mold with sauce—the pepper strips will show through in a colorful pattern. Serve the remaining sauce separately.

Chaud-froid of Stuffed Chicken
(POULARDE FARCIE EN CHAUD-FROID)

This is a spectacular dish for a buffet. The preparations are fairly elaborate, but they can be completed well ahead of time. In fact, the whole point of a dish coated in aspic or chaud-froid sauce is that it can be made in advance and hours later still remain moist under its decorative and protective coating.

4–5 pound (2 kg) chicken
6–7 cups (1.5–1.75 L) chicken stock (5)
¼ cup (60 ml) Madeira or sherry
salt
aspic (8) made with 1½ quarts (1.5 L) enriched stock from cooking the chicken, ½–1 ounce (15–30 g) gelatin, 2 carrots, green tops of 2 leeks, 2 celery stalks, 2 tomatoes, 7 ounces (200 g) beef, 3 egg whites, ¼ cup (60 ml) sherry, and salt and pepper
small can truffles OR several black olives
fresh chervil, tarragon, or parsley leaves
2 tomatoes

For the stuffing:
½ pound (250 g) lean cooked ham
⅓ cup (80 ml) of the aspic (above)
1 tablespoon Madeira or port wine
juice from the truffles—optional
⅓ cup (80 ml) heavy cream, lightly whipped
salt and pepper
pinch of grated nutmeg

For the chaud-froid sauce:
¼ ounce (7 g) gelatin
½ cup (125 ml) of the aspic (above)
velouté sauce (16) made with 2 cups (500 ml) chicken stock (5), 3 tablespoons (45 g) butter, 3 tablespoons (25 g) flour, and salt and pepper
¼ cup (60 ml) heavy cream

trussing needle and string

Serves 6–8.

At least 1 day ahead cook the chicken: Truss the bird, put it in a pot, and add chicken stock (5) to cover, the ¼ cup (60 ml) Madeira or sherry, and salt. Bring to a boil, reduce the heat, and poach, uncovered, 1¼–1½ hours or until tender. Let cool in the liquid, drain, and chill.

Make the aspic (8) with the resulting stock and set aside to cool.

For the stuffing: Work the ham twice through the fine blade of a grinder, then pound it in a mortar with a pestle to a smooth paste, and stir in ⅓ cup (80 ml) of the aspic. Alternatively, grind the ham with the aspic to a paste in a blender or a food processor. Cool the ham in a bowl set over a pan of ice, stirring often. Add the 1 tablespoon Madeira or port and the truffle liquid. Stir in the ⅓ cup (80 ml) cream 1 tablespoon at a time. Season to taste with salt and pepper and nutmeg. (Note: The ham may already be salty enough.)

Cut the trussing strings from the bird, then remove all the skin, and discard it. With a sharp knife remove the breasts and cut them into diagonal slices. Cut away the breastbone and ribs of the bird and discard them. Pile the stuffing in the chicken, mounding it well, then re-form the breasts on top of the filling. Set the bird on a rack over a tray to catch drips and chill thoroughly.

For the chaud-froid sauce: Sprinkle the ¼ ounce (7 g) gelatin over ½ cup (125 ml) of the aspic in a small pan and let stand 5 minutes or until spongy. Make the velouté sauce (16), add the cream, and bring back just to a boil. Melt the gelatin over very low heat and stir it into the warm velouté sauce. Taste for seasoning and adjust if necessary.

Set the sauce over a pan of ice and chill, stirring occasionally, until it is on the point of setting. Spoon it over the chilled chicken. (Note: If the sauce sets before the chicken is completely coated, melt it over low heat, chill again, and start over.) Chill the chicken until the coating is thoroughly set.

For decoration: Slice the truffles or cut shapes from the black olives. Pour boiling water over the chervil, tarragon, or parsley, leave

1 minute to soften the leaves and to set the color, then drain. Peel and seed the tomatoes and cut shapes from the flesh. Set these decorations in a saucer of the cool but still liquid aspic; it will make them stick to the chilled chicken. Arrange the shapes on the chicken as flowers or in any decorative pattern you like.

Pour about 1 cup (250 ml) of the remaining aspic into a metal bowl, set over ice, and chill, stirring occasionally, until it is on the point of setting. Immediately spoon it over the chicken to coat it all, chill until set, and repeat once or twice more. Chill the chicken thoroughly. Pour a thin layer of aspic to cover the bottom of a large platter and chill; pour the rest of the aspic into a baking dish and chill.

To finish: Carefully set the chicken on the aspic-lined platter. Run a knife around the edge of the other dish of aspic and turn it out onto a damp sheet of waxed paper. Cut crescents or triangles out of the aspic and arrange them around the edge of the platter. Chop any remaining aspic and spoon it around the chicken.

This dish can be kept in the refrigerator for several hours; let it come to room temperature before serving.

Veal Paupiettes with Lemon Stuffing
(PAUPIETTES DE VEAU FARCIES AU CITRON)

Veal paupiettes, ready-stuffed, rolled, and tied, are sold in most French butcher shops, but you can easily duplicate them yourself. They have long been known in English as veal birds. Serve them with fresh pasta.

8 (about 1½ pounds or 750 g) thin veal scallops
1 teaspoon oil
2 tablespoons (30 g) butter

1 cup (250 ml) dry white wine
1½ cups (375 ml) white veal stock (4)
2 shallots, chopped
bouquet garni (1)
salt and pepper
3 tomatoes, peeled, seeded, and cut into strips
2 tablespoons chopped parsley
¼ cup (60 ml) heavy cream

For the stuffing:
4 tablespoons (60 g) butter
2 medium onions, chopped
1 cup (140 g) fresh bread crumbs
grated zest of 2 lemons
1 tablespoon chopped parsley
salt and pepper
squeeze of lemon juice
1 egg, beaten to mix

heavy thread or fine string

SERVES 4.

Put the scallops between two sheets of waxed paper and pound them with a rolling pin to ¼ inch (6 mm) thick.

For the stuffing: Melt 2 tablespoons (30 g) of the butter in a small pan and cook the onions until soft but not brown. Add the remaining butter, heat until melted, and stir the mixture into the bread crumbs. Add the lemon zest and parsley and season to taste with salt and pepper and lemon juice. Stir in the egg. Spread the stuffing on the scallops, roll them, and tie in neat bundles with thread or string.

In a skillet or sauté pan heat the oil and butter and brown the "birds" on all sides. Add the wine, stock, shallots, bouquet garni, and salt and pepper. Bring to a boil, cover, and simmer 20–25 minutes or until the veal is tender. Remove the strings and bouquet garni. Arrange the paupiettes on a platter or on plates and keep warm.

Reduce the sauce to a coating consistency, add the tomato strips, and simmer 1–2 minutes. Stir in the parsley and cream and bring just to a boil. Taste for seasoning, adjust if necessary, and spoon the sauce over the paupiettes.

Claude Vauguet

Stuffed Breast of Veal
(POITRINE DE VEAU FARCIE)

For stuffing the veal, Claude often uses more hard-cooked eggs and leaves them whole so that when the meat is carved there is a bull's-eye of egg in the center of each slice.

3–3½ pound (1.5–1.75 kg) unboned piece of breast of veal
salt and pepper
1 tablespoon oil
2 tablespoons (30 g) butter
1 medium onion, quartered
1 carrot, quartered
1 stalk celery, cut in 2-inch (5 cm) lengths
1 cup (250 ml) white wine
1½ cups (375 ml) brown veal stock (2)
1 garlic clove, crushed
bouquet garni (1)

For the stuffing:
1 onion, finely chopped
2 tablespoons (30 g) butter
1 pound (500 g) veal, ground
1 cup (140 g) fresh bread crumbs
2 garlic cloves, finely chopped
grated zest of 1 lemon
2 tablespoons chopped parsley
pinch of grated nutmeg
salt and pepper
2 eggs, beaten to mix
2 hard-cooked eggs, sliced
2 ounces (60 g) cooked ham, cut in julienne strips

heavy thread or fine string

Serves 6.

For the stuffing: Cook the onion slowly in the butter until soft but not brown. Stir into the ground veal with the bread crumbs, garlic, lemon zest, parsley, nutmeg, and plenty of salt and pepper. Stir in

73

the beaten eggs and beat the stuffing well. Sauté a teaspoon of stuffing in a little oil, taste for seasoning, and adjust if necessary.

Bone the veal breast and reserve the bones. Spread the veal out, fat side down, and season with salt and pepper. Spread the stuffing over the meat, leaving a 1-inch (2.5 cm) border uncovered. Top the stuffing with the sliced eggs and scatter ham strips over the eggs. Roll the veal and tie neatly in a cylinder with string. Preheat the oven to 350° F (175° C).

In a heatproof casserole brown the veal in oil and butter, then remove it. Replace with the onion, carrot, and celery, cover, and cook gently 5–7 minutes or until softened. Add the reserved veal bones, set the meat on top, and add the wine, stock, garlic, bouquet garni, and salt and pepper. Bring to a boil on top of the stove, cover, and braise in the preheated oven 2–2½ hours or until tender. Remove the meat from the pan. Boil the cooking liquid until reduced to about 1½ cups (375 ml), strain, and skim off any fat. Taste for seasoning and adjust if necessary. Remove the strings.

The veal may be served hot or cold. It should be carved and arranged in overlapping slices to show the colorful stuffing. Use the cooking juices warm as a sauce. Or chill them until jelled, then chop to garnish the cold meat.

Pork Chops Dijonnaise
(CÔTES DE PORC DIJONNAISE)

This preparation is good for veal chops as well as for pork. When lean bacon is not available, Canadian bacon is an excellent alternative (sauté it only briefly).

1 tablespoon oil
⅓ pound (150 g) piece lean bacon, cut into small strips (lardons)

18 small onions, scalded and peeled
four 1-inch-thick (2.5 cm) pork chops
1 tablespoon (8 g) flour
½ cup (125 ml) dry white wine
1 cup (250 ml) white veal (4) or chicken (5) stock
bouquet garni (1)
salt and pepper
¼ cup (60 ml) heavy cream
2 tablespoons Dijon mustard, or to taste
1 tablespoon chopped parsley

SERVES 4.

In a large skillet heat the oil, add the bacon, and cook, stirring occasionally, until browned and most of the fat is rendered. Take out, add the onions, and brown them. Take them out, add the chops, and brown on both sides. Remove them and discard all but 2 tablespoons (30 g) of the fat in the skillet. Sprinkle in the flour and cook until bubbling. Add the wine, stock, bouquet garni, and salt and pepper and bring to a boil, stirring.

Replace the chops and bacon in the skillet, cover, and simmer on top of the stove or in a 350°F (175°C) oven 25–30 minutes. Add the onions and cook 15 minutes or until the chops and onions are tender. Remove the chops and keep warm on a platter or plates.

If necessary, boil the sauce to reduce it until well flavored. Add the cream, bring back just to the boil, and take from the heat. Stir in the mustard at the last minute and heat but do not boil. (NOTE: If overheated, mustard becomes bitter.) Discard the bouquet garni, taste for seasoning, and spoon the sauce and onions over the chops. Sprinkle with chopped parsley and serve.

Beef Stroganoff
(BOEUF STROGANOFF)

For this recipe, the less expensive tail of the beef fillet is often used. Stroganoff can be cooked in a chafing dish at the table, providing the burner gives a strong heat. Quick cooking is important so the meat will remain rare and tender.

> 5 tablespoons (80 g) butter, clarified
> 1 onion, sliced
> ½ pound (250 g) mushrooms, sliced
> 1½ pound (750 g) beef fillet, cut into 2- × ½- × ½-inch (5 × 1.25 × 1.25 cm) pieces
> 1 tablespoon paprika—optional
> ¼ cup (60 ml) brandy
> salt and pepper
> 1 cup (250 ml) sour cream

SERVES 4.

In a skillet or chafing dish heat 2 tablespoons (30 g) of the butter and cook the onion over medium heat until golden brown. Add the mushrooms and cook, stirring, until tender. Take them out and wipe out the pan.

Roll the beef strips in paprika. In half the remaining butter fry a few strips over high heat 1–2 minutes, stirring, so they brown on the outside and remain rare in the center. (NOTE: If the pan is not hot enough, or too much meat is cooked at once, the beef will stew rather than brown.) Remove the browned strips and fry the rest in small quantities, adding more butter when the pan is dry.

Return all the meat to the pan, heat well, pour the brandy over it, and flame. Add the onion, mushrooms, and salt and pepper and cook 1–2 minutes until very hot. Add the sour cream, bring almost to a boil, taste for seasoning, and serve. (NOTE: If the sour cream comes to a boil, it will separate.)

Claude Vauguet

Crown Roast of Lamb
(CARRÉ D'AGNEAU EN COURONNE)

*The vegetables for garnishing this crown roast of lamb are carefully
"turned" with a knife to give each piece a perfect oval shape. This
work is not just for show since uniformly shaped vegetables also cook
evenly.*

3–4 tablespoons oil
3 racks of lamb
salt and pepper
1 cup (250 ml) dry white wine
2 cups (500 ml) brown beef (3) or brown veal (2) stock

For the garnish:
2 pounds (1 kg) baby carrots, peeled, or large carrots, peeled and
quartered
2 pounds (1 kg) small new potatoes, peeled, or 4 large potatoes,
peeled and quartered
2 teaspoons sugar
6 ounces (180 g) butter
salt and pepper
2 pounds (1 kg) baby Brussels sprouts or green beans

paper frills—optional

SERVES 8–10.

Heat the oil in a large roasting pan and quickly sear the fat side
of each rack of lamb. Tie them in a circle into a crown roast, season,
and return to the roasting pan. Preheat the oven to 400°F (200°C).

For the garnish: Trim the carrots and potatoes into uniform olive
shapes. Bring the carrots to a boil with the sugar, 2 tablespoons (30 g)
of the butter, salt and pepper, and water to cover; simmer 10–15
minutes or until tender. Then boil rapidly until nearly all the liquid
has evaporated. In a sauté pan or shallow casserole melt 5 tablespoons
(80 g) of the butter and put in potatoes. Cover and cook over high
heat, shaking the pan occasionally, for 15–20 minutes or until tender.
Sprinkle with salt and pepper. Cook the sprouts or beans in boiling
salted water until just tender. Drain, refresh with cold running water,

and transfer to a pan with the remaining butter.

Roast the lamb 15–20 minutes or until a meat thermometer registers 140°F (60°C) for rare or 160°F (70°C) for medium-rare meat. Transfer the roast to a platter, remove the strings, and keep warm. Discard the fat in the roasting pan, pour in the white wine and stock, and deglaze the pan, boiling until the gravy is well reduced. Taste for seasoning and strain into a sauceboat. Reheat the vegetables if necessary and pile into the center of the crown. Decorate the platter with any remaining vegetables and top each chop bone with a paper frill.

Braised Celery
(CÉLERIS BRAISÉS)

French chefs "peel" celery stalks just like carrots, with a vegetable peeler—a quick way to remove the strings. Braised celery is especially good with veal.

1 head of celery
1 tablespoon oil
2–3 slices bacon, diced—optional
1 onion, diced
1 carrot, diced
about 1 cup (250 ml) white veal stock (4)
bouquet garni (1)
salt and pepper
1 teaspoon arrowroot or potato starch
1 tablespoon water
1 tablespoon chopped parsley

SERVES 4.

Separate the celery into stalks and wash. Cut off the leaves, strip away the tough strings, and cut the celery into 3-inch (7.5 cm) lengths. Blanch in boiling water 1 minute and drain. Preheat the oven to 350°F (175°C).

In a sauté pan or casserole heat the oil and fry the bacon until the fat is rendered. Add the onion and carrot and cook over low heat 5–7 minutes until soft. Put the celery on top and add the stock (4), bouquet garni, and salt and pepper. (NOTE: If using bacon, salt may not be needed.) Cover and braise in the preheated oven ¾–1 hour or until the celery is tender. Add more stock during cooking if the pan gets dry. The celery can be cooked 1–2 days ahead and kept, covered, in the refrigerator.

Reheat celery mixture if necessary on top of the stove. Remove and keep warm. Strain the cooking liquid into a pan and reduce if necessary to about ¾ cup (185 ml). Mix the arrowroot and water to a paste. Stir in enough of the paste to thicken the liquid slightly. Taste this sauce for seasoning and adjust if necessary. Spoon over the celery, transfer to a serving dish or plates, sprinkle with parsley, and serve.

Cucumber Gratin
(CONCOMBRES AU GRATIN)

Cooked cucumbers are a delicious garnish for fish, chicken, or veal, but they can be watery. Remember to remove as many of the seeds as possible when trimming the cucumber pieces.

    3 large cucumbers (about 2 pounds or 1 kg)
    3 tablespoons (45 g) butter
    salt and pepper
    1 tablespoon water

> Mornay sauce (14) made with 1 cup (250 ml) béchamel sauce
> (13), ¼ cup (25 g) grated Gruyère OR ¼ cup (30 g) grated
> Parmesan cheese, and 1 teaspoon Dijon mustard
> 2 tablespoons (10 g) grated Gruyère OR 2 tablespoons (15 g)
> Parmesan cheese

SERVES 4.

Peel the cucumbers. Cut them into 2-inch (5 cm) lengths, divide each in four lengthwise, and trim the pieces to olive shapes. Or, cut the cucumbers in half lengthwise, scoop out the seeds, and slice into ½-inch (1.25 cm) crescents. In a sauté pan melt 2 tablespoons (30 g) of the butter and add the cucumbers, salt and pepper, and water. Cover and cook over low heat, shaking occasionally, for 5–7 minutes or until nearly tender.

Make the Mornay sauce (14). Spoon a little of it into a shallow buttered baking dish, add the cucumber pieces, and coat with the remaining sauce. Sprinkle with the 2 tablespoons of grated cheese. Melt the remaining 1 tablespoon (15 g) of the butter and sprinkle on top. The dish can be prepared up to 24 hours ahead, but the cucumbers should then be slightly undercooked to allow for reheating. Keep, covered, in the refrigerator.

To finish: If the cucumbers are still warm, brown under the broiler. If cold, reheat in a preheated 400°F (200°C) oven 10–12 minutes until browned.

Stuffed Eggplant Imam Bayeldi
(AUBERGINES FARCIES IMAM BAYELDI)

Imam bayeldi means "the priest fainted." The question is whether he did so from pleasure, from overeating, or from horror at the cost of this dish involving the lavish use of the valuable Mediterranean commodity olive oil.

2 medium eggplants OR 4 baby eggplants, unpeeled
salt and pepper
½ cup (125 ml) olive oil
5 ripe tomatoes, peeled
3 medium onions, chopped
2 garlic cloves, chopped
2 tablespoons chopped parsley

SERVES 4.

Preheat the oven to 425°F (220°C). Cut the stems from the eggplants and halve them lengthwise. With the tip of a knife cut around the edges inside the skins and slash the centers. Sprinkle the cut surfaces with salt and leave 30 minutes to draw out the bitter juices. Wipe with paper towels. Put the eggplant in an oiled baking dish, pour on ¼ cup (60 ml) of the olive oil, and bake in the preheated oven 20–25 minutes or until tender. Remove from the oven, gently scoop out the flesh, and chop it; reserve the shells.

Seed and chop 3 of the tomatoes; slice the remaining 2 tomatoes. Heat 3 tablespoons of the oil and sauté the onions until golden brown. Add the garlic and cook 1 minute; then take from the heat and stir in the chopped tomatoes and salt and pepper. Cook 15 minutes or until most of the liquid has evaporated. Stir in the eggplant pulp and cook 3–4 minutes more. Take from the heat, add the chopped parsley, and taste for seasoning.

Season the eggplant shells and return them to the baking dish. Spoon in the filling and garnish each shell with 3 or 4 tomato slices pushed into the filling vertically at regular intervals. Sprinkle with the remaining 1 tablespoon oil and bake in the preheated oven 15–20 minutes or until the filling is hot. Serve hot, warm, or at room temperature. The eggplants can be kept, covered, 2–3 days in the refrigerator, and they reheat well.

Sautéed Potatoes
(POMMES SAUTÉES)

Browned potatoes cook much more evenly if they are boiled first and then sautéed until crisp.

> 3–4 medium (1½ pounds or 750 g) potatoes
> salt and pepper
> 2 tablespoons oil and 2 tablespoons (30 g) butter (for frying)
> 1 tablespoon chopped parsley

SERVES 4.

Scrub the potatoes and put them, unpeeled, in cold salted water. Cover, bring to a boil, and simmer 15–20 minutes or until just tender. Drain, peel, and cut in chunks while they are still warm. In a large skillet heat the oil and butter and add the potatoes. They will quickly absorb all the fat and should toast in the pan until brown and crisp. Turn them occasionally so they brown on several sides, though it is impossible to brown them entirely evenly. Before serving, sprinkle with salt and pepper and chopped parsley.

Souffléed Oranges
(ORANGES SOUFFLÉES)

It's important that egg whites used in soufflés be very stiff. When students ask Claude how long to beat them, he answers, "until you're very tired."

> 4 large navel oranges

pastry cream (**34**) made with 3 egg yolks, 2 tablespoons (25 g) sugar, 2 tablespoons (15 g) flour, grated zest of 1 orange, 1 cup (250 ml) milk, 1 vanilla bean OR ½ teaspoon vanilla extract, and 3 tablespoons Grand Marnier or other orange liqueur

5 egg whites

2 tablespoons (25 g) sugar

powdered sugar (for dusting)

pastry bag with large star tip—optional

SERVES 4.

Cut the whole oranges in half crosswise. Scoop out the flesh without piercing the rind. Make the pastry cream (**34**), stirring the orange zest in with the flour and adding the Grand Marnier off the heat at the end.

Half an hour before serving, preheat the oven to 400°F (200°C). Heat the soufflé base until very hot but not boiling. Beat the egg whites until stiff, add the 2 tablespoons (25 g) sugar, and continue beating until glossy. Stir a quarter of the whites into the orange pastry cream, then add this to the remaining whites, and fold together as lightly as possible. Pipe the soufflé mixture into the orange halves or spoon it in. Bake in the preheated oven 5 minutes or until puffed and brown. Sprinkle heavily with powdered sugar and return to the oven 1–2 minutes or until glazed. Serve at once.

Snow Eggs

(OEUFS À LA NEIGE)

Custard sauce must be made with care to avoid curdling. If you overcook it, warns Claude, you'll end up with sweet scrambled eggs.

Swiss meringue (**40**) made with 4 egg whites and ⅔ cup (135 g) sugar

custard sauce (35) made with 2 cups (500 ml) milk, a vanilla bean
OR 1 teaspoon vanilla extract, 4 egg yolks, and ⅓ cup (65 g)
sugar

For the caramel:
⅓ cup (65 g) sugar
3 tablespoons water

SERVES 4.

Make the Swiss meringue (40). Before folding in the last of the
sugar, whisk until the mixture forms long peaks when the whisk is
lifted.

Fill a sauté pan or shallow saucepan half full with water and
bring it almost to a boil. Dip a large metal spoon into the water and
then shape an oval of meringue with it. Tap the handle of the spoon
sharply on the edge of the sauté pan to detach the meringue. Add
4–5 of these "eggs" to the water and poach them 30 seconds or until
firm, turning them once. Lift out with a slotted spoon and drain on
paper towels. Continue with the remaining meringue.

Make the custard sauce (35) and strain into a serving bowl.

To finish: When the custard is cool, arrange the meringue eggs
on top of it. For the caramel: Heat the sugar and water over low heat
until the sugar dissolves; then boil steadily to a golden caramel. Let
cool until it stops bubbling, then drizzle it in crisscross trails across
the eggs. The dessert can be made up to 4 hours ahead and stored in
the refrigerator. If the caramel is kept too long, it will liquify.

Albert Jorant

ALBERT JORANT enters a classroom quickly, with a light step, and winks to all. He's usually already rubbing his hands together in anticipation of the day's baking. *Pâtissier* Jorant can make a pound of *pâte brisée* in exactly two minutes, twenty seconds. As he works, he never stops talking. Jorant says, with a big smile, that this is so no one in the audience will fall asleep, but there's little chance of that in his fast-moving demonstrations. He is a born teacher, but remarks that, after fifty years in the business, it's only natural that he has a few tips to pass on.

His career began in 1930 when, at thirteen, he was apprenticed to a caterer. Jorant worked for the next four years without a single day off, sometimes, for banquets, laboring forty-eight hours nonstop —not an easy life for an undersized boy who was so small he had to stand on the foot-locker that held his modest possessions to get himself up to table height to work. Once, during these years, he injured two fingers on his right hand. They took a long time to heal, but he stayed on duty and used his left hand so that now he is almost ambidextrous. This is a capability he encourages students to develop for many reasons; just one—Chef Jorant can beat egg whites twice as long as anyone else.

At seventeen, Jorant was accepted for his first job as an assistant chef. He was a navy cook during his military service and then returned to baking and catering, as a chef and manager, until 1952 when he went into the business on his own. Twenty years later, he turned demonstrator and instructor, spending four years at the Cordon Bleu in Paris before joining La Varenne in 1976. He insists that, though there may be many good methods in *pâtisserie*, students should follow *his* methods because they are the best. His students are firm believers because even the impressive displays of the best *pâtisseries* of Paris pale before Jorant's ethereal cakes, perfect tarts, or his delicately decorated *petits fours*.

Chef Pâtissier Albert Jorant, with student assistant, demonstrates making a tart shell.

Albert Jorant's Choices

FIRST COURSES

Spinach Tourte, p. 88
Vegetable Julienne Pie, p. 89

MAIN COURSES

Striped Bass in Pastry, p. 91
Lamb Chops in Puff Pastry, p. 92

YEAST DOUGHS

Brioches, p. 94
Swiss Brioche, p. 95

MOLDED DESSERTS

Coffee Bavarian Cream, p. 97
Chocolate Charlotte, p. 98

CAKES

Strawberry Mousse Cake, p. 100
Rolled Sponge Cake with Chocolate Filling, p. 101
Almond Meringue Cake, p. 102

PETITS FOURS

Sweet Puff Pastries, p. 104
Wells of Love, p. 105
Florentines, p. 106

Spinach Tourte
(TOURTE AUX ÉPINARDS)

This closed pie is from Provence, which produces more vegetables, and seemingly more good vegetable recipes, than any other part of France.

> pie pastry (**24**) made with 2 cups (260 g) flour, ¼ pound (125 g) unsalted butter, 2 egg yolks, 1 tablespoon oil, 1 teaspoon salt, and 5–6 tablespoons cold water
> 1 egg, beaten with ½ teaspoon salt (for glaze)

> *For the filling:*
> 1½ pounds (750 g) spinach
> 2 tablespoons (30 g) butter
> ¼ pound (125 g) mushrooms, sliced
> salt and pepper
> pinch of grated nutmeg
> ⅓ cup (80 ml) heavy cream

> *8-inch (20 cm) tart pan with removable bottom*

SERVES 6.

Make the pie pastry (**24**) and chill 30 minutes.

Preheat the oven to 400°F (200°C). Lightly butter the tart pan. Roll out about half the dough, line the pan with it, and chill until firm. Prick the base with a fork. Line the dough with aluminum foil, fill with dried beans or rice, and bake in the preheated oven 10–12 minutes or until the pastry is set and beginning to brown. Remove the beans and foil and bake the shell 3–4 more minutes or until the bottom is firm. Remove from the oven and let the shell cool slightly.

For the filling: Remove the spinach stems, wash the leaves well, and boil 2–3 minutes in a large pan of boiling salted water. Refresh under cold running water, drain, squeeze out all excess liquid, and chop. In a saucepan melt the butter, add the mushrooms, and cook slowly 5–10 minutes or until tender. Add the spinach, salt and pepper, and nutmeg and cook together, stirring, until any remaining liquid in the spinach has evaporated. Stir in the cream, taste for seasoning, and adjust if necessary.

88

Remove the shell from the pan, set it on a baking sheet, and spoon the spinach filling into it. Carefully brush the rim and outside edge of the shell with the egg glaze. Roll out the remaining dough to a 9-inch (23 cm) round. Place the round of dough over the bottom shell, overlapping the outside edge, press to stick the two layers together, and trim. Glaze the top of the tourte with the egg glaze. The top can be decorated with leaves or flowers cut from the remaining dough scraps; glaze the decorations. Prick the top several times to let any steam escape. Bake in the hot oven 35–40 minutes or until brown. Serve it hot. The tourte is best eaten the day it is baked.

Vegetable Julienne Pie
(TARTE À LA JULIENNE DE LÉGUMES)

Pastry chefs insist that the proportions for a dough must be followed to the letter, but a filling can be varied at will. So in this recipe use other vegetables if you wish, or replace the julienne mixture entirely with grated cheese for a cheese quiche.

>*For the dough:*
3–3¼ cups (390–420 g) flour
1 package dry yeast OR 1 cake (15 g) compressed yeast
½ cup (125 ml) lukewarm milk
3 eggs
1½ teaspoons salt
¼ pound (125 g) butter, softened

>*For the filling:*
2 carrots
white part of 3 large leeks
½ pound (250 g) mushroom caps
⅓ pound (150 g) ham, thinly sliced

3 tablespoons (45 g) butter
salt and pepper

For the custard:
3 eggs
1 cup (250 ml) heavy cream
salt and pepper
pinch of grated nutmeg

two 8–9-inch (20–23 cm) pie or round cake pans

SERVES 8–10.

For the dough: Sift the smaller quantity of the flour (3 cups or 390 g) into a bowl, make a well in the center, and crumble in the yeast. Pour ¼ cup (60 ml) of the milk over the yeast and let stand 5 minutes or until dissolved. Add the remaining milk, the eggs, and salt. Beat with one hand, using a quick chopping motion, gradually drawing in enough flour to make a dough that is soft and slightly sticky, then knead the dough by slapping it against the sides of the bowl or on a marble slab for 5 minutes or until it is very elastic. Beat in the softened butter. Transfer to an oiled bowl and cover with a damp cloth. Let rise in a warm place 1–1½ hours or until doubled in bulk.

For the filling: Cut the carrots, leeks, mushroom caps, and ham into thin julienne strips 1½ inches (4 cm) long. In a sauté pan melt the butter and add the carrots, leeks, and salt and pepper. Cover and cook over low heat, stirring often, for 15 minutes. Add the mushrooms and continue cooking, stirring often, about 10 minutes more or until all the vegetables are tender. Stir in the ham and taste for seasoning.

For the custard: Beat the eggs with the cream, salt and pepper, and nutmeg.

Preheat the oven to 400°F (200°C). Knead the dough lightly to knock out the air. Butter the pans, divide the dough in half, and set it in the pans. With the oiled back of a spoon or your fingers, flatten the dough to line the pans. Cover the bottoms of the pans with the julienne mixture and pour the custard on top. Leave in a warm place to rise 15 minutes. Bake in the preheated oven 40–50 minutes or until the pastry is brown and the custard is set. Serve hot or warm.

Albert Jorant

Striped Bass in Pastry
(LOUP EN CROÛTE)

Brioche used as an encasing pastry must be rolled quickly to prevent the butter added to the dough from melting. Chef Jorant says his cold hands are an advantage, and during hot weather when they're warmer than usual, he plunges them into ice water to lower their temperature.

brioche dough (28) made with 4 cups (520 g) flour, 2½ teaspoons salt, 1 tablespoon sugar, 1 package dry yeast OR 1 cake (15 g) compressed yeast, 2 tablespoons lukewarm water, 5 eggs, and 5 ounces (150 g) butter

4–5-pound (2 kg) whole striped bass, scaled and cleaned but head left on

salt and pepper

1–2 tablespoons oil

1 egg, beaten with ½ teaspoon salt (for glaze)

fresh herbs—thyme, basil, parsley

hollandaise sauce (20) made with 6 ounces (180 g) butter, 3 tablespoons water, 3 egg yolks, salt, white pepper, and the juice of ½ lemon

SERVES 6–8.

Make the brioche dough (28) and chill at least 4 hours or overnight. Wash the bass and dry thoroughly inside and out. Cut off the fins and trim the tail to a "V." Season the fish inside and out. Cut a paper pattern the same shape as the bass but a little larger. Butter a baking sheet.

Divide the dough in half. Roll out one half a little longer than the length of the fish, set it on the prepared baking sheet, and brush with oil. Set the fish on top and trim the dough, leaving a 1-inch (2.5 cm) border all around. Brush the border with the egg glaze. Add the trimmings to the remainder of the dough, roll it out a little longer than the length of the fish, and cut a second fish shape, this time using the paper pattern. Brush the top of the fish with oil, put a bunch of fresh herbs in the stomach, and cover the fish with the dough. Press the edges of dough together to seal and push in all around to neaten the shape. Brush the entire surface with the glaze and decorate the pastry fish with a mouth and eye made from the trimmings of dough. With scissors snip half way through the dough to make a pattern of scales and mark lines on the tail. Let the brioche fish rise in a warm place 30–45 minutes or until slightly puffed.

Preheat the oven to 425°F (220°C). Bake the fish in the preheated oven 10 minutes, turn the oven down to 375°F (190°C), and bake 30–35 minutes more or until a skewer inserted in the center for 30 seconds is hot to the touch when withdrawn.

Meanwhile, make the hollandaise sauce (**20**).

Transfer the fish to a large platter and serve the sauce separately. At the table: Cut all around the edge to loosen the top crust and lift it off to disclose the fish. Lift off the top fillet of the fish from the bone as usual and serve a piece of brioche crust with each portion. Remove the bone to reach the bottom fillet and cut the bottom crust also into serving pieces.

Lamb Chops in Puff Pastry
(CÔTELETTES D'AGNEAU EN CUIRASSE)

Glaze the surface of puff pastry evenly, without letting any egg drip down the side. Drips of glaze glue the layers together and prevent the dough from rising properly. The chef compares glaze to paint: "Brush on two layers to get an even coat."

> puff pastry (**27**) made with ¾ pound (350 g) unsalted butter, 2 cups (260 g) all-purpose flour, 1 cup (120 g) cake flour, 1½ teaspoons salt, 1½ teaspoons lemon juice, and ¾–1 cup (185–250 ml) cold water
> 8 rib lamb chops
> 2 tablespoons oil
> salt and pepper
> 8 slices cooked ham
> 1 egg, beaten with ½ teaspoon salt (for glaze)

For the duxelles:
½ onion, finely chopped
2 tablespoons (30 g) butter
½ pound (250 g) mushrooms, finely chopped
½ garlic clove, crushed—optional
1 tablespoon chopped parsley
salt and pepper

2½–3-inch (6–7.5 cm) plain round cookie cutter
½–¾-inch (1.25–2 cm) fluted round cookie cutter
pastry wheel
paper frills (optional)

SERVES 4–8, depending on the rest of the menu.

Make the puff pastry (**27**) and chill. Trim the fat and meat from the ends of the chops to expose about 1 inch (2.5 cm) of bone; scrape the bone ends clean. In a skillet heat the oil and brown the chops over high heat allowing 30 seconds on each side. Season and leave to cool. Cut 16 rounds of ham the same size as the chops.

For the duxelles: In a skillet cook the onion slowly in the butter until soft but not brown. Add the mushrooms and cook over high heat, stirring, until all the moisture has evaporated. Add the garlic and cook 30 seconds longer. Stir in the chopped parsley with salt and pepper to taste and let cool.

Roll out the dough to a 16- × 18-inch (40 × 45 cm) rectangle and cut in half crosswise. Brush one half with the egg glaze and set 8 rounds of ham on top in 2 parallel lines, ¾–1 inch (2–2.5 cm) from the edge. Spread each round with duxelles, using half the mixture, and top with a chop, arranging the chops so their bones protrude over the edge of the dough. Spread the remaining duxelles on the chops and top with rounds of ham. Cover the chops with the second sheet of dough, letting it fall loosely down between them. (NOTE: Do not stretch it.) Using a ball of dough dipped in flour, press it down firmly to seal the layers of dough around the chops. Cut around each chop with a pastry wheel leaving a ½-inch (1.25 cm) border; press the edges to seal. Brush with egg glaze and set on a dampened baking sheet.

Pile the dough trimmings one on top of another and roll out to a thin sheet. Cut eight ¼-inch (6 mm) strips, twist them, and arrange one around the edge of each chop. Cut 24 small rounds with the fluted cutter and arrange 3 of them on each chop. Brush the decorations with egg glaze, make a hole in the center with the point of a knife to allow steam to escape, and chill the chops 15 minutes. They can be prepared up to 6 hours ahead and kept, covered, in the refrigerator.

To finish: Preheat the oven to 425°F (220°C). Bake until puffed and brown, allowing 12–15 minutes for medium-rare and 15–18 minutes for well-done. Put paper frills on the bones and serve at once.

Brioches
(BRIOCHES)

Anyone who has seen Chef Jorant shaping brioches gasps at his dexterity. He rolls a ball of dough, forms the topknot, and then plops the brioche in its mold. The whole operation takes fifteen seconds. His pressing and rolling with the sides of his hand is quite literally a "tour de main." The method described here is slower but easier.

brioche dough (28) made with 4 cups (520 g) flour, 2½ teaspoons
    salt, 2 tablespoons (25 g) sugar, 1 package dry yeast OR 1
    cake (15 g) compressed yeast, 2 tablespoons lukewarm water,
    6–7 eggs, and ½ pound (250 g) unsalted butter
1 egg, beaten with ½ teaspoon salt (for glaze)

*15 small brioche pans OR 2 large brioche pans (6 inches or 15 cm
    in diameter)*

Makes 15 small or 2 large brioches.

Make the brioche dough and chill thoroughly. Butter the brioche pans. Knead the dough lightly to knock out the air and divide it into 15 pieces (for individual brioches) or in half (for large loaves). Pinch off one third of each piece of dough and shape both large and small pieces into balls. Set a large ball in each buttered brioche pan, cut a deep cross in the top, and crown it with a smaller ball or "head" of dough.

NOTE: The heads of brioches often slip sideways or subside into the lower part of the dough during baking. To help prevent this, the shaped brioches should be chilled at least 12 hours and up to 36 hours in the refrigerator, or they can be frozen for up to 3 weeks.

Let the brioches rise at room temperature, allowing about 30 minutes for small ones or 1–1¼ hours for large loaves, or until they almost fill the pans. (NOTE: Chilled brioches may already have risen sufficiently in the refrigerator.) Preheat the oven to 425°F (220°C). Brush the risen brioches with the egg glaze and bake in the preheated oven, allowing 15–20 minutes for small brioches or until they are well browned and give a hollow sound when tapped on the bottom. For large loaves, after 15 minutes turn down the oven heat to 375°F (190°C) and continue baking 30–40 minutes or until they start pulling away from the sides of the pan and give a hollow sound when tapped on the bottom. Cool on a wire rack. Baked brioches can be kept 2–3 days in an airtight container, or they can be frozen.

Swiss Brioche
(BRIOCHE SUISSE)

Chef Jorant warns against using too much salt in sweet pastry. If you must use salted butter, be sure to cut the quantity of salt added to the dough by half.

> brioche dough (28) made with 2 cups (260 g) flour, 1¼ teaspoons salt, 1 tablespoon sugar, ½ package dry yeast OR ½ cake (7 g) compressed yeast, 1 tablespoon lukewarm water, 3–4 eggs, and ¼ pound (125 g) unsalted butter
> ½ cup (60 g) chopped candied fruits

½ cup (70 g) raisins or currants
2 tablespoons rum or Cointreau
1 egg, beaten with ½ teaspoon salt (for glaze)
¼ cup (60 ml) apricot glaze (38)

For the frangipane:
3 tablespoons (45 g) butter
¼ cup (50 g) sugar
1 egg yolk
⅓ cup (50 g) almonds, blanched, peeled, and ground
½ teaspoon rum

8–9-in (20–23 cm) round cake pan

SERVES 5–6.

Make the brioche dough, let rise, and refrigerate several hours or overnight so it will be easy to roll out. Moisten the candied fruits and the raisins or currants with the rum or Cointreau and leave to macerate about 30 minutes.

For the frangipane: Cream the butter, gradually beat in the sugar, and continue beating until light and soft. Gradually beat in the egg. Stir in the ground almonds and rum.

Roll out half the dough into a thin 10-inch (25 cm) circle and line the pan with it. Prick lightly with a fork. Roll out the rest of the dough to a thin rectangle. Spread it with a thin layer of frangipane. Drain the fruit and spoon it evenly onto the layer of frangipane. Roll it up, from a short end, like a jelly roll, and cut the roll into slices ¾ inch (2 cm) thick. Arrange the slices flat in the lined pan so they barely touch each other. Trim the dough, lining the pan to about 1 inch (2.5 cm) below the top of the pan. Cover with a towel and let rise 2–3 hours at room temperature.

Preheat the oven to 400°F (200°C). Brush the brioche with the egg glaze and bake 35–45 minutes or until it is golden brown and pulls away from the sides of the pan. When cool, brush with melted apricot glaze (38). The brioche can be kept 2–3 days in an airtight container, or it can be frozen.

Albert Jorant

Coffee Bavarian Cream
(BAVAROIS AU CAFÉ)

When making a Bavarian cream, be especially careful to add the dis-solved gelatin to hot custard. Once, when a student couldn't under-stand why his Bavarian cream fell apart, Chef Jorant actually pulled strings of gelatin from the mixture. The gelatin had been added to cool custard and was never completely incorporated.

¼ ounce (7 g) gelatin
¼ cup (60 ml) cold water
custard sauce (**35**) made with 2 cups (500 ml) milk, 1 vanilla
      bean OR ½ teaspoon vanilla extract, 2½–3 teaspoons instant
      coffee, 6 egg yolks, and 6 tablespoons (80 g) sugar
½ cup (125 ml) heavy cream, lightly whipped
Chantilly cream (**36**) made with ½ cup (125 ml) heavy cream,
      2 teaspoons sugar, and ½ teaspoon vanilla extract

3–4 cup (750 ml–1 L) plain mold
pastry bag with medium star tip

SERVES 8–10.

Sprinkle the gelatin over the water in a small bowl and leave 5 minutes or until spongy. Rinse the mold with cold water.

Make the custard sauce (**35**), adding the coffee as the milk re-heats. When thickened, take from heat at once and strain into a metal bowl. Add the softened gelatin to the hot custard, stir until com-pletely dissolved, and leave to cool, stirring occasionally.

When cool, set the custard mixture over a bowl of ice water. Keep stirring the custard; when it is cold to the touch and you feel it becoming thicker, it is beginning to set. Now add the whipped cream by folding it in gently. Pour the mixture into the prepared mold. Cover and leave in the refrigerator 1–2 hours or until firmly set. The dessert can be made up to 24 hours ahead, but it tends to stiffen and must be brought to room temperature before serving.

To finish: Not more than 2 hours before serving, make the Chantilly cream. Unmold the dessert. Run a knife around the edge of the mold, pull the mixture away from the side of the mold with a finger to release the airlock, and dip the bottom of the mold in a bowl of hot water for a few seconds. Set a platter upside down on top and turn the mold and platter over. Give a sharp shake so the dessert falls onto the platter. Using the pastry bag with a star tip, decorate the edge of the Bavarian cream with rosettes of the Chantilly cream.

Chocolate Charlotte
(CHARLOTTE AU CHOCOLAT)

Fashions come and go, but charlottes remain popular both with classic and nouvelle-cuisine chefs.

> 12–15 ladyfingers (**31**) made with ½ cup (65 g) flour, a pinch of salt, 2 eggs, ¼ cup (50 g) sugar, ¼ teaspoon vanilla extract, and powdered sugar
> ¼ ounce (7 g) gelatin
> ¼ cup (60 ml) water
> 6 ounces (180 g) semisweet chocolate, chopped
> custard sauce (**35**) made with 2 cups (500 ml) milk, 2 teaspoons instant coffee, 5 egg yolks, and ¼ cup (50 g) sugar
> 1 tablespoon rum
> ½ cup (125 ml) heavy cream, lightly whipped
>
> *For decoration:*
> ¼ pound (125 g) semisweet chocolate, chopped
> Chantilly cream (**36**) made with ¾ cup (185 ml) heavy cream, 1–2 teaspoons sugar, and 1 teaspoon rum
>
> *1½-quart (1.5 L) capacity charlotte mold*
> *pastry bag with medium star tip*

SERVES 8–10.

Make the ladyfingers (31).

Line the bottom of the charlotte mold with a circle of waxed paper. Line the sides of the mold with ladyfingers, trimming them to a slight taper so they fit tightly.

Sprinkle the gelatin over the water in a small bowl and leave 5 minutes or until spongy. Melt the 6 ounces (180 g) of chocolate in a heatproof bowl over a pan of hot water.

Make the custard sauce (35), adding the coffee as the milk re-heats. When thickened, take it from heat at once and strain into a metal bowl. Add the softened gelatin to the hot custard and stir until completely dissolved. Then slowly stir the custard into the melted chocolate and leave to cool, stirring occasionally.

When the custard is cool, add the rum, set the bowl over ice, and stir until the mixture starts to set. Fold in the lightly whipped cream and pour the mixture into the lined charlotte mold. (NOTE: The mixture must be fairly thick or it will soak the ladyfingers.) Cover and chill at least 2 hours or until completely set. The charlotte can be made 1 day ahead and kept, covered, in the refrigerator, but the gelatin mixture tends to stiffen, so let it stand 1–2 hours at room temperature before serving.

For the decoration: Melt the ¼ pound (125 g) chocolate in a heatproof bowl over a pan of hot water. Spread chocolate evenly about ⅛ inch (3 mm) thick over an 8-inch (20 cm) square of waxed paper and, when it is on the point of setting, mark it into 1-inch (2.5 cm) diamonds with a sharp knife. Chill until set; then peel away the paper.

To finish: Make the Chantilly cream. Trim the ladyfingers level with the top of the charlotte and unmold it onto a platter. Peel off the waxed-paper circle. Use the pastry bag and star tip to decorate the bottom and the top with rosettes of Chantilly cream and top them with chocolate diamonds.

Strawberry Mousse Cake
(GÉNOISE À LA MOUSSE DE FRAISES)

Many recipes using génoise call for cutting it into very thin, even layers. The secret is a long, serrated knife and a light sawing motion.

génoise (**29**) made with ¾ cup (95 g) flour, tiny pinch of salt, 4 tablespoons (60 g) butter, 4 eggs, ⅔ cup (135 g) sugar, and ½ teaspoon vanilla extract

For the strawberry mousse:
½ ounce (15 g) gelatin
7 tablespoons water
2 cups (200 g) strawberries
½ cup (100 g) sugar
Chantilly cream (**36**) made with 1½ cups (375 ml) heavy cream, 1½ tablespoons sugar, and 1 teaspoon vanilla extract

pastry bag with medium star tip

SERVES 8.

Make the génoise (**29**) and split horizontally into 3 layers.

For the strawberry mousse: Sprinkle the gelatin over ¼ cup (60 ml) water in a small bowl and leave 5 minutes or until spongy. Save 8 small perfect strawberries; purée the rest in a blender or food processor or work through a strainer. Make a syrup by bringing the ½ cup (100 g) sugar and 3 tablespoons water just to a boil. Add the softened gelatin to the hot syrup, stir until dissolved, and leave to cool, stirring occasionally. Stir in strawberries purée. Make the Chantilly cream. Set the strawberry mixture in a bowl of ice water and stir until it is cold to the touch and starts to thicken. Fold in one third of the Chantilly cream and remove the mixture from the bowl of ice water. (NOTE: When the mousse is on the point of setting, it must be spread on the génoise immediately.)

Sandwich the layers of génoise with the mousse. Spread more mousse on top. Spread Chantilly cream on the sides and transfer to a serving plate. The cake can be made up to 24 hours ahead, but the filling tends to stiffen so bring it to room temperature before serving.

To finish: Decorate the cake with rosettes of whipped cream, using a pastry bag fitted with a medium star tip. Top each rosette with a strawberry.

Rolled Sponge Cake with Chocolate Filling
(GÉNOISE ROULÉE À LA GANACHE)

Chef Jorant sometimes makes twice the amount of chocolate ganache given here and uses it both for filling and for frosting. A double-rich result.

For the cake:
5 tablespoons (45 g) flour
¼ cup (35 g) cornstarch
3 eggs
3 egg yolks
⅓ cup (65 g) sugar
½ teaspoon vanilla extract

For the chocalate ganache filling:
⅓ cup (80 ml) heavy cream
¼ pound (125 g) semisweet chocolate, chopped
powdered sugar (for dusting)

SERVES 6–8.

Butter a sheet of parchment paper and put it on a large baking sheet. Preheat the oven to 375°F (190°C).

For the cake: Sift the flour with the cornstarch. Whisk the eggs, egg yolks, and sugar in a bowl until mixed. Set the bowl over a pan of hot but not boiling water and whisk until the mixture is light and fluffy and leaves a ribbon trail when the whisk is lifted. Take from the heat and continue beating until cool. Alternatively, beat the eggs, yolks, and sugar in an electric mixer; heat is not necessary with the mixer method. Stir in the vanilla, then fold in the flour as lightly as possible, in 2 or 3 batches.

Spread the cake batter on the prepared baking sheet in a thin layer, forming a rectangle about 16- × 20-inches (40 × 50 cm). Bake in the preheated oven 10–12 minutes or until very lightly browned. (NOTE: Do not overcook the cake, or it will crack.) Take the cake from the oven and cover at once with a dish towel to prevent steam escaping. This ensures that the cake can be rolled without cracking. Leave to cool; then turn the cake with the dish towel onto a rack and peel off the paper.

For the filling: Scald the cream. Take from the heat, add the chocolate, and stir until melted. Leave to cool; then beat 5 minutes so the filling is light and very smooth.

Trim the edges of the cake, spread the cake with the filling, then roll it, using the dish towel for support. Trim the ends diagonally, dust the roll with powdered sugar, and transfer to a platter for serving. The cake is best eaten the day it is made, or it can be frozen.

Almond Meringue Cake
(GÂTEAU PROGRÈS)

Nut meringue with praline butter cream is a classic combination in French pâtisserie. The filling might be flavored with coffee or chocolate in addition to the praline. For these variations, use either 2–3 teaspoons instant coffee dissolved in 1 tablespoon hot water or 3 ounces (90 g) melted semisweet chocolate.

For the meringue layers:
½ cup (65 g) hazelnuts
½ cup (75 g) whole blanched almonds
Swiss meringue (40) made with 4 egg whites, ⅔ cup (135 g) sugar, and ¼ teaspoon vanilla extract

For the praline butter cream:
praline (39) made with ½ cup (90 g) whole unblanched almonds
    and 6 tablespoons (80 g) sugar
butter-cream frosting (33) made with 3 egg yolks, 7 tablespoons
    (90 g) sugar, ¼ cup (60 ml) water, and 6 ounces (180 g)
    unsalted butter
powdered sugar (for dusting)
½ cup (75 g) blanched almonds, peeled, toasted, and chopped

pastry bag with ½-inch (1.25 cm) plain tip
paper piping cone—optional

SERVES 8–10.

For the meringue layers: Preheat the oven to 350°F (175°C). Toast the hazelnuts and whole blanched almonds 8–12 minutes or until browned. Let cool slightly and then rub the hazelnuts with a rough cloth or against a sieve to remove the skins. In a blender, a food processor, or nut grinder, grind the almonds and hazelnuts to a powder a few at a time. Butter and flour as many baking sheets as you need for space, and mark three 9-inch (23 cm) circles in the flour, using a pan lid as a guide. Turn down the oven heat to 250°F (120°C).

Make the Swiss meringue (**40**) and fold in the ground nuts. Using the pastry bag, pipe in 9-inch (23 cm) rounds on the prepared baking sheets and bake the meringues in the preheated oven 40–50 minutes or until crisp, dry, and just beginning to brown. Trim the rounds neatly with a sharp knife while still warm, then transfer to a rack to cool. They can be kept up to 1 week in an airtight container.

For the praline butter cream: Make the butter cream (**33**) and beat in the praline (**39**).

To finish: Sandwich the meringue layers with about two-thirds of the butter cream. Spread more butter cream on the top and sides, reserving 2–3 tablespoons. Dust the top of the cake generously with powdered sugar and press the toasted chopped almonds around the sides. Set the cake on a platter. Put the reserved butter cream in a paper piping cone and pipe the word "Progrès" across the top of the cake. The cake should be assembled one day ahead so the flavor will mellow and the cake will be easier to slice. It keeps well in the refrigerator 2–3 days and can be frozen.

Sweet Puff Pastries
(FEUILLETÉS SUCRÉS)

A marvelous way to use up puff-pastry scraps. These little pastries are delicious enough to warrant making a fresh batch of dough, too.

> puff pastry (**27**) made with ½ pound (250 g) butter, 1⅓ cups (175 g) all-purpose flour, ⅔ cup (80 g) cake flour, 1 teaspoon salt, 1 teaspoon lemon juice, and ½–¾ cup (125–185 ml) water
> OR the equivalent in puff-pastry trimmings
sugar (for rolling and sprinkling)

Make the puff pastry and chill thoroughly. Shape the pastries according to the recipes that follow. Set on a dampened baking sheet and chill 15 minutes. Preheat the oven to 425°F (220°C). Bake the pastries 8–12 minutes or until puffed and brown. (NOTE: Watch carefully as they burn very easily.) Transfer to a rack to cool. The pastries can be kept 1–2 days in an airtight container, or they can be frozen, baked or unbaked.

Beef Tongues (LANGUES DE BOEUF):

Roll out the prepared dough to a sheet ¼ inch (6 mm) thick and cut out 3-inch (7.5 cm) rounds with a fluted pastry cutter. Roll each one to an oval, transfer to a dampened baking sheet, and brush with lightly beaten egg white. Sprinkle generously with sugar, chill, and bake as described above. Makes about 24 langues de boeuf.

Butterflies (PAPILLONS):

Give the last 2 turns to the puff pastry on a surface sprinkled with sugar instead of flour. Chill until firm.

Roll out the prepared dough to a 10- × 16-inch (25 × 40 cm) rectangle and trim the edges. Cut the dough into 3 strips each about

3 inches (7.5 cm) wide. Arrange them one on top of the other. With the handle of a knife make a deep crease lengthwise down the center, then with a sharp knife cut the dough into ¼-inch (6 mm) slices. Twist each one at the crease and transfer to a dampened baking sheet. Chill and bake as described above. Makes 30–35 papillons.

Wells of Love

(PUITS D'AMOUR)

Because these little shells of puff pastry needn't rise very much, they are another ideal way to use leftover scraps of dough. Press the scraps together, keeping the layers horizontal, chill well, then roll out again.

puff pastry (see pp. 229–231)
1 egg beaten with ½ teaspoon salt (for glaze)
½ cup (150 g) red currant jelly

1½-inch (4 cm) and 1-inch (2.5 cm) fluted round pastry cutters

MAKES about 2 dozen pastries if you use the full recipe on p. 230.

Make the puff pastry (**27**) and chill. Preheat the oven to 425°F (220°C).

Roll out the dough ⅛ inch (3 mm) thick and prick it well. Stamp out rounds with the 1½-inch (4 cm) cutter. Transfer half the rounds to a baking sheet sprinkled with water and brush them with the egg glaze. Cut a circle from the center of each of the remaining rounds with a 1-inch (2.5 cm) cutter and set the rings on top of the rounds on the baking sheet. Press the rings gently to seal them to the round below. Brush them with glaze.

Chill the pastries 15 minutes, then bake in the preheated oven 12–15 minutes or until puffed and brown. Transfer them to a rack to cool. While still warm lift out the "hat" which has formed in the center, and if necessary scoop out any uncooked dough with a spoon.

(NOTE: If the dough was rolled to a thin enough sheet, this should not be necessary.) The pastries can be baked 3–4 days ahead and stored in an airtight container, or they can be frozen, baked or unbaked.

Not more than 6–8 hours before serving, melt the red-currant jelly, let it cool until almost set and spoon it into the pastries.

Florentines
(FLORENTINES)

Because chocolate is sensitive to heat, it will lose its gloss if overheated. Melt it over hot but not boiling water and never over direct heat.

> 3 tablespoons (45 g) butter
> ½ cup (125 ml) heavy cream
> ⅔ cup (135 g) sugar
> ¼ cup (30 g) candied cherries, soaked in hot water, drained, and quartered
> ¾ cup (90 g) candied orange peel, finely chopped
> 1¼ cups (190 g) blanched almonds, finely chopped
> ½ cup (45 g) sliced blanched almonds
> ⅓ cup (45 g) flour
> 8 ounces (250 g) semisweet chocolate, chopped
>
> *3-inch (7.5 cm) plain round cookie cutter*
> *cake decorating comb—optional*

MAKES about 30 florentines.

Grease and lightly flour 2 baking sheets and preheat the oven to 350°F (175°C).

Bring the butter, cream, and sugar slowly to a boil. Take from the heat and stir in the cherries, orange peel, chopped and sliced almonds, and flour. Drop teaspoonsful of the mixture onto the prepared baking sheets, leaving plenty of room for them to spread. Flatten each with a wet fork.

Bake in the preheated oven 5–6 minutes. Take from the oven and, with the cookie cutter, pull in the edges of each cookie. Return to the oven and bake 5–6 minutes longer or until lightly browned at the edges. Cool slightly on the baking sheets; then lift off with a sharp knife and transfer to a rack.

Melt the chocolate on a heatproof plate over a pan of hot water. Stir with a wooden spoon until smooth. Spread the smooth undersides of the cookies with chocolate and, if you like, when it is on the point of setting, mark it with wavy lines using a cake decorating comb or a knife with large serrations on the blade, such as a "tomato knife."

Anne Willan

MOST PEOPLE would tire from following Anne Willan around for just a day—and would be exhausted after a week in her footsteps. At twenty-one, she graduated from Cambridge with a master's degree in economics. A year later, in 1960, she had completed the most advanced course at London's Cordon Bleu Cookery School and was offered a post as teacher and demonstrator, which she filled for two years. Then it was on to the Paris École du Cordon Bleu for a year to earn its *grand diplôme*. This was followed by more teaching as well as catering and a job as entertainment advisor at the Château de Versailles. Her next move was to the United States, where she worked first as an associate editor of *Gourmet* magazine and later as food editor for the *Washington Star* and became an American citizen.

In 1975, having returned to Paris, Anne opened France's first bilingual cooking school—La Varenne. With her indefatigable spirit presiding, L'École de Cuisine La Varenne flourishes, giving the lie to all the raised French eyebrows that once expressed doubt at the very idea of an Anglo-American—and a woman at that—daring to start a serious cooking school on hallowed ground. Now, the very chefs who may have scoffed accept invitations to give guest demonstrations at the school.

Anne breezes through the kitchens of La Varenne, noting everything. "That soufflé mixture is just the right consistency; it will rise," she says, commending a student from across the room. She seems to keep track of every detail at the school, from the French accounting system to the state of the herbs in the window boxes.

Anne Willan

A journalist and a superb, incredibly informed teacher, Anne is also an author. She was editor-in-chief of the twenty-volume *Grand Diplôme Cooking Course*. Her own first book, *Entertaining Menus*, was published in 1974, followed by *Great Cooks and Their Recipes* in 1977. Several more books are under way, as are plans for demonstration tours in Europe and continued tours in the United States. Anne is married to Mark Cherniavsky, an economist with the World Bank, and is bringing up two young children. She explains her ability to accomplish so much: "I'm fortunate enough to be a part of two marvelous teams—one at home and one at work."

Anne Willan.
In Paris, Anne is known as the
Directrice *of La Varenne.*

Anne Willan's Choices

FIRST COURSES

Turnip Soup, p. 111
Stuffed Mushrooms La Varenne, p. 112
Rich Cheese Soufflé, p. 112
Shrimp Pâté, p. 114

MAIN COURSES

Shrimp Newburg, p. 114
Fish Fricassee with Limes and Ginger, p. 116
Chicken Fricassee with Mushrooms and Baby Onions, p. 117
Chicken Suprêmes La Varenne, p. 119
Duck Steak with Green Peppercorns, p. 120
Veal Scallops with Roquefort, p. 121
Beef Fillet Cherniavsky, p. 122
Noisettes of Lamb with Celery Root, p. 123

VEGETABLES AND SALADS

Eggplant Terrine, p. 125
Potatoes Darphin, p. 127

DESSERTS

Hot Orange Soufflé, p. 128
Norwegian Cream, p. 129
Chocolate Snowball, p. 130
Trifle, p. 131

Anne Willan

Turnip Soup
(POTAGE FRENEUSE)

Don't turn up your nose at turnips. You'll find that this soup is a delicacy.

3 tablespoons (45 g) butter
3–4 medium (1 pound or 500 g) turnips, thinly sliced
1 medium potato, sliced
4–5 cups (1–1.25 L) white veal stock (4) or milk, or a combination of the two
salt and pepper
3–4 tablespoons (45–60 g) butter

For the croûtons:
3–4 slices firm, white bread, with crusts removed, diced
2 tablespoons oil and 2 tablespoons (30 g) butter (for frying)

SERVES 6.

In a heavy-bottomed pan melt the 3 tablespoons (45 g) butter, add the turnips, and press a piece of buttered waxed paper on top. Cover with the lid and cook gently, stirring occasionally, for 10–15 minutes or until the turnips soften. (NOTE: Do not allow them to brown.) Add the potato, 4 cups (1 L) of the stock or milk, and salt and pepper. Cover and simmer 15–20 minutes or until the vegetables are very tender.

Work the soup through a food mill or sieve, or purée it in a blender. Add more liquid if necessary—the soup should be creamy in consistency but not thick. Taste it for seasoning and adjust if necessary. The soup can be made 2 days ahead and kept, covered, in the refrigerator, or it can be frozen.

For the croûtons: Fry the diced bread in the oil and butter until golden brown and drain.

To finish: Bring the soup to a boil, take it from the heat, and stir in the butter a small piece at a time. Ladle the soup into bowls and pass the croûtons separately.

Stuffed Mushrooms La Varenne
(CHAMPIGNONS FARCIS LA VARENNE)

This is an old recipe that was recorded in the mid-17th century by the great chef La Varenne himself.

½ pound (250 g) uncooked veal or boned breast of chicken
1 pound (500 g) large mushrooms
2 tablespoons chopped chives
salt and pepper
2 egg yolks
3 tablespoons (45 g) butter
squeeze of lemon juice

SERVES 4 as a first course or accompaniment to a main dish.

Preheat the oven to 350°F (175°C). Stem the mushrooms. Work the veal or chicken and the mushroom stems twice through the fine blade of a grinder. Add the chives and plenty of salt and pepper and stir in the egg yolks to bind the mixture. Spoon the stuffing into the mushroom caps, pressing to mound it. The mushrooms can be prepared 6–8 hours ahead.

To finish: Melt the butter in a baking dish, arrange the mushrooms in it, and bake them in the preheated oven, basting often, for 25–30 minutes or until they are tender and the stuffing has browned. Sprinkle with lemon juice and serve hot.

Rich Cheese Soufflé
(SOUFFLÉ RICHE AU FROMAGE)

This recipe is risky, as only a small amount of potato starch is used to stabilize the cream, cheese, and butter. But the result is spectacular—the lightest imaginable cheese puff.

1 cup (250 ml) heavy cream
1 tablespoon (10 g) potato starch
1 tablespoon (15 g) butter
5 egg yolks
½ cup (60 g) grated Parmesan cheese
½ cup (50 g) grated Gruyère cheese
salt and pepper
pinch of dry mustard
8 egg whites

1½-quart (1.5 L) soufflé dish

SERVES 4–6.

Butter the soufflé dish generously. In a heavy saucepan put the cream, potato starch, and butter and heat gently, stirring, until the sauce thickens. Take at once from the heat or the sauce will separate. Stir in the egg yolks and cheeses, reserving 2 tablespoons (10 g) of the Gruyère to sprinkle on top of the soufflé. Heat gently, stirring, until the mixture thickens slightly again. Do not overcook it, or the cheese will form strings. Take from the heat and add salt and pepper and mustard. The mixture should be highly seasoned to compensate for the blandness of the egg whites. The soufflé base can be prepared up to 3 hours ahead and kept, covered with wet waxed paper, to prevent a skin from forming.

To finish the soufflé: Preheat the oven to 425°F (220°C). Beat the egg whites until stiff, in a copper bowl if possible. Heat the cheese mixture until hot to the touch. (NOTE: Do not let it cook into strings.) Add about a quarter of the egg whites and stir until well mixed. Then add the cheese mixture to the remaining egg whites and fold together as lightly as possible. Gently pour into the prepared soufflé dish, sprinkle with the remaining 2 tablespoons of Gruyère, and bake in the preheated oven 12–15 minutes, or until the soufflé is puffed and browned. Serve at once.

Shrimp Pâté
(PÂTÉ DE CREVETTES)

A simple standby in which the full flavor of the shrimp comes through. Try it also with fresh crab meat.

> 1 pound (500 g) cooked, peeled shrimp
> juice of ½ lemon
> ¼ pound (125 g) butter
> 2 tablespoons sherry or Madeira
> salt and pepper
> pinch of grated nutmeg
> hot toast (for serving)

SERVES 4.

Work the shrimp, with the lemon juice, a few at a time in a food processor or blender; they should be coarsely chopped, not puréed. Cream the butter, stir in the chopped shrimp, and season to taste with sherry or Madeira, salt and pepper, and nutmeg.

Pile the pâté in individual ramekins or a serving crock, cover tightly, and chill. If to be kept more than 3–4 hours, smooth the top and add a thin layer of clarified butter to seal the pâté before chilling. The pâté can be made up to 2 days ahead. Serve with hot toast.

Shrimp Newburg
(CREVETTES NEWBURG)

The style of shrimp Newburg, with its rich cream sauce, is typically French, though its origin is American. Shrimp Newburg is cooked the same way as lobster Newburg, which was created at Delmonico's restaurant in the 1890s and called lobster Wenburg. The name changed to Newburg after a disagreement between Mr. Wenburg and Mr. Delmonico.

1½ pounds (750 g) cooked, peeled shrimp
¼ pound (125 g) butter
½ teaspoon paprika
salt and pepper
⅓ cup (80 ml) brandy OR ½ cup (125 ml) Madeira
2 cups (500 ml) heavy cream
6 egg yolks

For the rice pilaf:
3 tablespoons (45 g) butter
1 onion, finely chopped
1½ cups (300 g) long-grained rice
3 cups (750 ml) water
salt and pepper

1-quart (1 L) ring mold

SERVES 4.

For the rice pilaf: In a heavy-bottomed pan melt 2 tablespoons (30 g) of the butter and cook the onion until soft but not brown. Add the rice and sauté, stirring about 2 minutes until the grains look transparent. Add the water and salt and pepper. Top with a round of buttered paper, cover, and bring to a boil. Lower the heat and simmer on top of the stove or in a preheated 350°F (175°C) oven for exactly 18 minutes. If the liquid has evaporated but the rice is not cooked, add more water and cook a few more minutes until tender. Let the pilaf cool 10 minutes. Stir with a fork, add the 1 remaining tablespoon (15 g) of the butter and taste for seasoning. Butter the mold and fill it with rice, pressing it down lightly. Keep warm.

In a sauté pan or chafing dish, melt 3 tablespoons (45 g) of the butter and add the shrimp. Sprinkle with paprika, and salt and pepper, cover, and heat gently 2–3 minutes. Add the brandy or Madeira and flame. Take from the heat and keep warm. Stir the cream into the egg yolks, add to the pan, and heat gently, shaking the pan until the sauce thickens. (NOTE: Do not allow it to get too hot, or it will curdle.) Off the heat add the remaining butter in small pieces, shaking the pan until incorporated. Taste for seasoning.

Turn the rice ring out onto a platter and spoon the shrimp into the center. Serve any remaining sauce separately.

Fish Fricassee with Limes and Ginger
(FRICASSÉE DE POISSON AU CITRON VERT ET AU GINGEMBRE)

Nouvelle cuisine presents many new combinations and this is one of the best—lightly poached fish in a stimulating sauce of lime and fresh ginger. The fricassee can also be prepared with eel, conger eel, sea bass, turbot, or any firm white fish.

> 2-pound (1 kg) piece of monkfish (anglerfish), with the bones
> fish stock (6) made with ½ onion, ½ tablespoon butter, the bones
>   from the fish, 2 cups (500 ml) water, 5 peppercorns, a bou-
>   quet garni (1), and ½ cup (125 ml) wine

> salt and pepper
> pinch of thyme
> juice of 1 lemon
> 1 tablespoon oil
> zest of 2 lemons
> 3 limes
> 1 cup (250 g) butter
> 4 green onions or scallions, thinly sliced
> ½ cup (125 ml) dry white wine
> 2 tablespoons heavy cream
> ½ teaspoon grated fresh ginger OR a pinch of powdered ginger
> 2 tablespoons chopped parsley

SERVES 4.

Fillet the fish and make the fish stock (6). Cut the fish into 2-inch (5 cm) chunks and wash thoroughly. Dry well, sprinkle with salt and pepper, thyme, lemon juice, and oil and leave to marinate about 1 hour.

Chop the lemon zest into the tiniest pieces possible and blanch it: Put in a saucepan of cold water, bring to a boil, and boil 3–4 minutes or until tender. Refresh under cold running water, drain thoroughly, and reserve. Peel the limes, cut the flesh into thin slices, and reserve.

In a sauté pan or shallow saucepan melt 1 tablespoon (15 g) of

the butter, add the green onions or scallions, and cook slowly 5–7
minutes or until soft but not brown. Add the fish and cook gently
with the onions, stirring, for 2–3 minutes. Add the wine and enough
fish stock to cover, bring to a boil, and simmer about 10 minutes or
until just tender. Remove the pieces of fish and reserve. The fish can
be cooked up to 24 hours ahead and kept, covered, in the refrigerator,
but then it should be slightly undercooked to allow for reheating.

   To finish: Reheat the fish if necessary in a little fish stock, taking
care not to overcook it. Drain and keep warm in a serving bowl. Boil
the fish cooking liquid and any remaining fish stock about 10 minutes
or until reduced to 2–3 tablespoons. Add the cream and reduce again.
Whisk in the remaining butter gradually in small pieces. Work sometimes over very low heat and sometimes off the heat, so that the butter
softens and thickens the sauce without melting. Stir in the blanched
lemon zest, the reserved lime slices, the ginger, and salt and pepper
to taste. Arrange the fish on a platter or plates. Add the chopped
parsley to the sauce and spoon over the fish. Serve immediately.

Chicken Fricassee with Mushrooms and Baby Onions
(FRICASSÉE DE POULET À L'ANCIENNE)

*This traditional fricassee, with its garnish of onions and mushrooms
and its sauce enriched with flour and egg yolk, is an interesting contrast to the new trends demonstrated in the preceding recipe for Fish
Fricassee with Limes and Ginger.*

   3 tablespoons (45 g) butter
   3½–4 pound (1.75 kg) roasting chicken, cut into 6 or 8 pieces
   2 tablespoons (15 g) flour
   2½–3 cups (625–750 ml) chicken stock (5)
   salt and white pepper
   bouquet garni (1)
   3 egg yolks

½ cup (125 ml) heavy cream
1 tablespoon chopped parsley

For the garnish:
16–18 baby onions, peeled
2 tablespoons (30 g) butter
½ cup (125 ml) chicken stock (5)
salt and pepper
½ pound (250 g) mushrooms, quartered

SERVES 4.

For the garnish: Put the onions in a pan with 1 tablespoon (15 g) of the butter, ¼ cup (60 ml) stock (5), and salt and pepper and cover tightly. Cook over low heat, shaking the pan occasionally, for 12–15 minutes or until tender. Put the mushrooms in a pan with the remaining 1 tablespoon (15 g) of butter and the remaining stock, add salt and pepper, cover tightly, and cook over very high heat until the liquid boils to the top of the pan. The onions and mushrooms can be cooked up to 2 days ahead and kept, covered, in the refrigerator.

In a sauté pan or skillet melt the butter and add the pieces of chicken, skin side down. Cook over low heat until the meat is stiffened and white; this should take about 10 minutes. Remove the pieces, add the flour, and cook, stirring, for 1–2 minutes until foaming but not brown. Add 2½ cups (625 ml) stock with salt and pepper and the bouquet garni and bring to a boil, stirring. Replace the pieces of chicken, cover, and cook over low heat on top of the stove or in a preheated 350°F (175°C) oven, stirring occasionally, 25–30 minutes or until tender. If the sauce gets too thick, add more stock.

Transfer the chicken to a platter or to plates and keep warm. Discard the bouquet garni, add the liquid from cooking the onions and mushrooms to the pan, and reduce the sauce, if necessary, until it coats a spoon. Then add the onions and mushrooms and heat thoroughly. Mix the yolks and cream in a bowl, stir in a little of the hot sauce, and stir this mixture back into the remaining sauce. Heat gently, shaking the pan, until the sauce thickens slightly. (NOTE: Do not boil or it will curdle.) Coat the chicken with the sauce, spoon the onions and mushrooms around it, and sprinkle with the parsley. Serve the remaining sauce separately.

Anne Willan

Chicken Suprêmes La Varenne
(SUPRÊMES DE VOLAILLE LA VARENNE)

The 17th-century chef François Pierre de la Varenne has been called the founder of French classical cooking. Among his creations is duxelles—the shallot-flavored mushroom purée used in so many recipes, including this one. A suprême is the boneless breast from one side of a chicken.

> 1 tablespoon heavy cream
> ½ pound (250 g) butter
> few drops lemon juice
> salt and pepper
> pinch of grated nutmeg
> 4 suprêmes
>
> *For the duxelles:*
> 4 ounces (125 g) fresh morels OR 1 ounce (30 g) dried morels
> ½ pound (250 g) mushrooms
> few drops lemon juice
> salt and pepper
> 1 tablespoon (15 g) butter
> 1 shallot, finely chopped
> 2 tablespoons heavy cream

SERVES 4.

For the duxelles: Wash fresh morels in several changes of water to remove all the sand. Soak dried morels 3–4 hours in cold water to cover and drain. Put the morels and mushrooms in a pan with a few drops lemon juice, salt and pepper, and water to cover. Cover and cook over high heat until the liquid boils to the top of the pan. Drain, reserving the liquid. Chop the morels and mushrooms until very fine or purée in a blender or food processor. Melt the 1 tablespoon (15 g) butter, add the chopped shallot, and cook slowly until soft but not brown. Add the mushroom purée and salt and pepper and cook over high heat, stirring, until nearly all the liquid has evaporated. Add the 2 tablespoons cream, bring to a boil, and reduce until thick but not dry.

For the sauce, boil the reserved mushroom cooking liquid until reduced to 2–3 tablespoons. Add the 1 tablespoon cream and reduce again. Gradually beat in 5 ounces (150 g) of the butter in small pieces. Work sometimes over very low heat and sometimes off the heat so the butter softens and thickens the sauce without melting. Add a few drops lemon juice, salt and pepper, and nutmeg to taste. Keep warm on a rack over warm, not boiling, water while cooking the suprêmes.

Season the suprêmes with salt and pepper. Heat the remaining butter in a sauté pan and cook the suprêmes over low heat 5–6 minutes on each side until tender but not brown. On a platter or plates arrange the suprêmes over the duxelles and coat with the sauce.

Duck Steak with Green Peppercorns
(MAGRET DE CANARD AU POIVRE VERT)

Magrets are boneless duck breasts. They are surprisingly like steak and can be combined with the same strong flavors suitable for beef.

breasts of 1 duck
1 tablespoon oil and 1 tablespoon (15 g) butter (for frying)
salt and pepper

For the sauce:
3 shallots, finely chopped
1½ cups (375 ml) red wine
2 tablespoons heavy cream
1 teaspoon green peppercorns, drained and crushed
1 tablespoon (15 g) butter

SERVES 2.

Use a sharp knife to remove the wishbone from the duck. Remove each breast by sliding the knife between the meat and the bone.

Cut off the wings. Leave the skin on the breasts if the layer of fat beneath it is not too thick, or remove both skin and fat, as you prefer.

In a heavy skillet, heat the oil and butter. Season the duck breasts with salt and pepper and fry over fairly high heat, allowing about 3 minutes on each side for rare meat. The meat should be well browned. The magrets can be served whole, halved diagonally, or sliced. Transfer to a platter or to plates and keep warm.

For the sauce: Add the chopped shallots to the pan and cook gently 1 minute. Add the wine, stir to dissolve the pan juices, and boil until reduced by half. Add the cream and green peppercorns and cook 2–3 minutes. Drain any juice from the duck into the sauce. Remove the sauce from the heat and add the 1 tablespoon (15 g) butter in 2–3 pieces, shaking the pan until the butter is incorporated. Taste for seasoning and adjust if necessary. Pour the sauce over the duck and serve.

Veal Scallops with Roquefort
(ESCALOPES DE VEAU AU ROQUEFORT)

Roquefort in a cooked dish gives an unexpected tang, but be sure not to over season since the cheese is quite salty.

1½ pounds (750 g) veal scallops
½ cup (65 g) flour
1½ tablespoons oil and 1½ tablespoons (20 g) butter (for frying)
1 cup (250 ml) heavy cream
½ cup (100 g) crumbled Roquefort cheese
pepper
salt—optional

SERVES 4.

Put each scallop between two sheets of waxed paper and pound it with a meat mallet or the side of a cleaver to flatten. Coat the scallops with flour, patting to remove the excess.

In a sauté pan or skillet heat the oil and butter and fry the scallops over medium heat until browned, allowing 2–3 minutes on each side. Arrange them on a platter or on plates and keep warm. Deglaze the pan with the cream and simmer until slightly reduced. Add the cheese and whisk constantly over low heat until smooth. Add pepper and salt if necessary and strain. Pour over the scallops and serve.

Beef Fillet Cherniavsky
(FILET DE BOEUF CHERNIAVSKY)

This dish, which can be prepared ahead, is a favorite of mine for dinner parties, so I gave it my married name.

Madeira sauce (11) made with 2 cups (500 ml) demi-glace sauce
    (10) and 3 tablespoons Madeira
3–4 pound (1.75 kg) beef fillet, trimmed and tied with string
salt and pepper
1 tablespoon oil
2 tablespoons chopped parsley

    For the stuffing:
2 shallots
4 ounces (120 g) bacon
1 pound (500 g) mushrooms, finely chopped
4 large tomatoes (2 pounds or 1 kg), peeled, seeded, and chopped
salt and pepper

SERVES 8–10.

Make the Madeira sauce (11). Preheat the oven to 450°F (230°C). Sprinkle the beef with salt and pepper. In a roasting pan on top of the stove heat the oil until very hot and brown the meat well on all sides. Roast the meat in the very hot oven 11 minutes. Remove and leave to cool.

For the stuffing: In a food processor chop the shallots and bacon together to a fine paste. In a skillet or sauté pan heat the shallot-and-bacon paste 1–2 minutes. Add the chopped mushrooms, mix well, and add the tomatoes, and salt and pepper. Cook over high heat, stirring often, for 15–18 minutes or until all moisture has evaporated. Taste for seasoning, adjust if necessary, and leave to cool completely.

When the beef fillet is cool, remove the strings. Carve it into ¾-inch (2 cm) slices, leaving each slice attached at the bottom. Spread 1–2 tablespoons stuffing on each slice and press the fillet back into its original shape. Wrap the beef in 2 layers of aluminum foil and tie with string. The beef can be prepared ahead up to this point and kept 1–2 days in the refrigerator. Keep any remaining stuffing in a bowl and store, covered, in the refrigerator.

To finish: If chilled, allow the beef to come to room temperature. Preheat the oven to 425°F (220°C). Put the beef, still wrapped in the foil, in a roasting pan and reheat in the oven 15 minutes or until the filling is hot. Leave the wrapped fillet in a warm place until ready to serve. Reheat any extra stuffing and spread it down the center of an oval platter. Unwrap the beef, saving the juices that escape, and set it on the platter on top of the stuffing. Add the juices to the sauce, bring to a boil, and spoon it over the beef. Sprinkle with the chopped parsley and serve immediately.

Noisettes of Lamb with Celery Root
(NOISETTES AU CÉLERI-RAVE)

A noisette is invariably small, being just the "nut" of tender meat from a thick loin chop, so it is generally given importance by being set on a croûton and topped with a vegetable such as a mushroom or an artichoke bottom. The celery-root cups in this recipe are unusual and a perfect complement to lamb. Watercress would be a suitable extra garnish.

2 medium celery roots
salt and pepper
4 tablespoons oil
4 tablespoons (60 g) butter
eight 1-inch-thick (2.5 cm) loin lamb chops, boned

For the croûtons:
8 slices firm, white bread
2 tablespoons oil and 2 tablespoons (30 g) butter (for frying)

For the sauce:
béarnaise sauce (**21**) made with 6 ounces (180 g) butter, 3 tablespoons vinegar, 3 tablespoons white wine, 10 crushed peppercorns, 3 chopped shallots, 1 tablespoon chopped tarragon
stems or leaves, 3 egg yolks, salt, white or cayenne pepper,
1 tablespoon chopped chervil or parsley, and 2 tablespoons
chopped tarragon leaves (to finish)
¼ cup (60 ml) Madeira or sherry
¼ cup (60 ml) brown veal stock (**2**)

SERVES 4.

Peel the celery roots and quarter them. Cut each piece into a
disk very slightly smaller than the noisettes and about ½ inch (1.25
cm) thick. With a melon baller scoop out the center to leave a shell
¼ inch (6 mm) thick, then bevel the edges with a knife to make a
smooth cup. Put the cups into a pan, cover with water, add salt, and
bring to a boil. Cook 20 minutes or until tender and drain.

For the croûtons: From the bread cut rounds slightly larger than
the noisettes. In a frying pan heat the oil and butter, fry the bread
rounds quickly on both sides until browned, and drain them.

Make the béarnaise sauce (**21**) and keep warm over hot water.
In a pan heat 2 tablespoons of the oil and 2 tablespoons (30 g) of the
butter, add the celery root cups, and heat thoroughly. Reheat the
croûtons in a low oven.

In a heavy frying pan heat the remaining 2 tablespoons oil and
2 tablespoons (30 g) butter. Sauté the noisettes over moderately high
heat, allowing 3–4 minutes on each side, or until browned but still
springy when pressed, showing they are pink in the center. Sprinkle
with salt and pepper after turning. Put the noisettes on the croûtons

and set a celery root cup on top of each noisette. Arrange on a platter or on plates and keep warm.

For the sauce: Pour off the fat in the pan and discard. Add to the pan the Madeira or sherry and the stock (2). Boil, scraping the bottom of the pan with a wooden spatula, until thickened and reduced to 2–3 tablespoons. Strain this reduction into the béarnaise sauce and stir well. Spoon the sauce into the celery-root cups and serve immediately.

Eggplant Terrine
(TERRINE D'AUBERGINES)

Vegetable terrines are very much in vogue. This dish, combining eggplant, zucchini, green peppers, and tomatoes with a good measure of olive oil and garlic, is like a molded ratatouille.

4 small eggplants (total weight, 2 pounds or 1 kg)
salt and pepper
⅓ cup (80 ml) olive oil
4 zucchini, sliced in thick rounds
3 onions, chopped
4 garlic cloves, finely chopped
2 red bell peppers, diced
3 green bell peppers, diced
3 tomatoes, peeled, seeded, and chopped
bouquet garni (1)
1 egg
⅓–½ cup (30–50 g) dry bread crumbs

For the tomato coulis:
1 pound (500 g) tomatoes, peeled, seeded, and chopped
salt and pepper

2-quart (2 L) terrine with lid

SERVES 6–8.

Preheat the oven to 425°F (220°C). Halve the eggplants lengthwise and score the flesh with a knife. Sprinkle with salt and let stand 30 minutes. Dry the eggplant, then bake in an oiled pan 15–20 minutes or until the flesh has softened somewhat. Remove the pulp with a spoon, being careful not to pierce the skin.

For the tomato coulis: In a heavy-bottomed saucepan, cook the tomatoes with salt and pepper over low heat, covered, for 10 minutes. Uncover and simmer, stirring occasionally, about 15 minutes or until very thick.

In a skillet heat 2 tablespoons of the oil and sauté the zucchini rounds until lightly browned.

In a large heavy-bottomed pan heat the remaining oil, add the onions, and cook slowly until soft but not brown. Add the eggplant pulp, tomato coulis, zucchini, garlic, peppers, tomatoes, and bouquet garni. Season with salt and pepper and cook, uncovered, for 25–30 minutes or until all the vegetables are tender and the mixture is thick. Discard the bouquet garni. Remove from the heat and stir in the egg and enough bread crumbs to make the mixture stiff but not dry. Taste for seasoning and adjust if necessary.

Preheat the oven to 350°F (175°C). Make small slits in the eggplant skins to flatten them if necessary. Oil the terrine generously and line it with the skins, purple sides outward. Spoon in the vegetable mixture. Cover the terrine and put in a water bath. Bring to a boil on top of the stove, then bake in the oven 1 hour or until firm. Cool about 15 minutes and unmold. Serve hot, warm, or cold.

Anne Willan

Potatoes Darphin
(POMMES DARPHIN)

I like to serve this potato cake with poultry dishes such as Chicken Fricassee with Mushrooms and Baby Onions (p. 117) or Duck Ragoût with Pears (p. 48).

2 pounds (1 kg) baking potatoes, peeled
2 tablespoons oil
4 tablespoons (60 g) butter
salt and pepper

7–8-inch (18–20 cm) heavy ovenproof frying pan

SERVES 4.

Cut the peeled potatoes into julienne strips and dry thoroughly on paper towels. (NOTE: Do not soak potatoes in water as this removes some of their starch, which is necessary in this dish to hold the potatoes together.) Spread the oil and half of the butter over the bottom and sides of the pan and press in a thick layer of potatoes. Dot with butter and sprinkle lightly with salt and pepper. Add the remaining potatoes, seasoning each layer lightly with salt and pepper. Cover the pan with buttered foil and top with the lid. Preheat the oven to 375°F (190°C).

Cook the potatoes over low heat 10 minutes or until the bottom is browned. To check, lift up one side of the potatoes with a metal spatula—you should smell browned butter. Then bake 30 minutes or until very tender. Loosen the base of the cake with a metal spatula and turn it out on a platter. Cut in wedges to serve.

Hot Orange Soufflé
(SOUFFLÉ CHAUD À L'ORANGE)

Rather like the Rich Cheese Soufflé (p. 112) made with so little flour, this orange mixture is extra light because it contains no flour at all.

    4 tablespoons (60 g) butter
    ⅔ cup (135 g) granulated sugar, in all
    ½ cup (125 ml) orange juice
    4 egg yolks
    grated zest of 1 orange
    5 egg whites
    powdered sugar (for dusting)
    1–2 tablespoons Grand Marnier—optional

1-quart (1 L) soufflé dish

SERVES 4.

Butter the soufflé dish, sprinkle with granulated sugar, and discard the excess. In a heavy-bottomed pan (not aluminum) heat the butter with ¼ cup (50 g) of the ⅔ cup sugar and the orange juice until the butter and sugar melt. Take from the heat and beat in the yolks one by one. Add the orange zest. Heat very gently, stirring constantly, until the mixture thickens to the consistency of heavy cream. (NOTE: Do not let it get too hot or it will curdle.) The soufflé can be prepared 3–4 hours ahead to this point. Keep, covered, at room temperature.

Twenty to thirty minutes before serving, preheat the oven to 425°F (220°C). Beat the whites until stiff, preferably in a copper bowl. Add the remaining sugar and beat 20 seconds longer or until glossy. Gently heat the orange mixture until hot to the touch, then stir in about a quarter of the egg whites. Add this mixture to the remaining whites and fold together as lightly as possible. Gently pour into the prepared dish and bake at once in the preheated oven 12–15 minutes or until puffed and brown. Dust the top with powdered sugar, sprinkle with Grand Marnier, and serve at once.

Anne Willan

Norwegian Cream
(CRÈME NORVÉGIENNE)

As the custard for this rich cream bakes, check to see that the water bath does not boil; if it gets too hot, the finished custard will be grainy rather than smooth.

3 tablespoons apricot jam
½ cup (125 ml) heavy cream
1 egg white
2 tablespoons (25 g) sugar
½ teaspoon vanilla extract
2 ounces (60 g) semisweet chocolate, grated

For the custard:
2 cups (500 ml) milk
3 tablespoons (35 g) sugar
1 vanilla bean OR ½ teaspoon vanilla extract
2 eggs
3 egg yolks

4 ramekins (1-cup or 250 ml capacity)
      OR *1-quart (1 L) soufflé dish*

SERVES 4.

Preheat the oven to 350°F (175°C). Melt the jam, spread in the bottom of the ramekins or soufflé dish, and cool.

For the custard: Heat the milk with the sugar until dissolved. Add the vanilla bean, cover, and leave to infuse over low heat for 10–15 minutes. Remove the vanilla bean. Beat the eggs and yolks until frothy and stir in the milk. If using vanilla extract, add it now. Leave to cool. Strain into the prepared ramekins and cover with foil.

Set the ramekins in a water bath, bring just to a boil on top of the stove, then bake 20–25 minutes for ramekins or 30–40 minutes for a soufflé dish, or until a knife inserted in the center of the custard comes out clean. Let cool; then chill. The custard can be cooked 48 hours ahead and kept, tightly covered, in the refrigerator.

Not more than 3 hours before serving, whip the cream. Whip the

129

egg white until stiff, add the sugar, and continue beating until glossy. Fold it and the vanilla into the whipped cream. Sprinkle the custards with half the grated chocolate, cover them completely with the whipped topping, and garnish with the remaining chocolate.

Chocolate Snowball
(BOULE DE NEIGE AU CHOCOLAT)

If you're going to eat dessert, why count calories? It is hard to imagine anything richer than this mold, made with almost equal weights of chocolate, butter, sugar, and eggs. A generous coating of whipped cream gives the snowball effect.

> 8 ounces (250 g) sweet chocolate, chopped
> ½ cup (125 ml) strong, black coffee
> > OR 2 teaspoons instant coffee dissolved in ½ cup (125 ml) warm water
> ½ pound (250 g) unsalted butter
> 1 cup (200 g) sugar
> 4 eggs, beaten to mix
> Chantilly cream (36) made with 1½ cups (375 ml) heavy cream, 1–2 tablespoons (12–25 g) sugar, and 2–3 teaspoons brandy
> candied violets

> *4–5-cup (1–1.25 L) charlotte mold or deep metal mold*
> *pastry bag with medium star tip*

SERVES 6–8.

Line the mold with a double thickness of foil. Preheat the oven to 350°F (175°C). In a heavy-bottomed pan melt the chocolate in the coffee over low heat. Add the butter and sugar a little at a time, stirring after each addition until melted. Heat until very hot but do not boil. Take from the heat and beat in the eggs a little at a time. Strain into the prepared mold and bake 30–40 minutes or until a thick crust has formed on top. The mixture will rise slightly, but will fall again as it cools. Let cool, then cover, and keep at least 3 days or up to 2 weeks in the refrigerator.

To finish: Not more than 3 hours before serving, run a knife around the mold and turn it out onto a platter. Peel off the foil—the dessert tends to stick and will look messy at this point. Make the Chantilly cream and with the pastry bag pipe rosettes onto the mold to cover it completely, so that no chocolate shows. Crown it with a single, larger, rosette and stud the top and sides with candied violets. Chill until served.

Trifle
(TRIFLE)

In Yorkshire where I grew up, this dessert is a perennial favorite. It is not a trifling dish at all, but a hearty mixture of cake, poached fruit, egg custard, and whipped cream. Fresh fruit poached in a light syrup is certainly best, but canned fruit will do.

a pound cake OR a sponge cake (30) made with ¾ cup (95 g) flour, a pinch of salt, 4 eggs, and ¾ cup (150 g) sugar
6 ounces (180 g) raspberry jam
½ cup (125 ml) sherry
1 pound (500 g) canned pears or peaches, drained and sliced
custard sauce (35) made with 3 cups (750 ml) milk, a vanilla bean OR 1 teaspoon vanilla extract, 4 eggs, 5 egg yolks, and ¾ cup (150 g) sugar
1 cup (250 ml) heavy cream, whipped until stiff
¼ cup (35 g) whole blanched almonds, toasted

1½-quart (1.5 L) glass bowl
pastry bag with medium star tip

SERVES 6–8.

Cut the cake in 3 layers, sandwich with raspberry jam, and cut into 1-inch (2.5 cm) squares. Put the squares in the bottom of the bowl, spoon in the sherry, and press down lightly. Arrange the drained fruit on top.

Make the custard sauce (35) and let cool to tepid. Pour the custard over the cake and fruit, cover, and chill.

Not more than 3 hours before serving, with the pastry bag cover the custard completely with small rosettes of whipped cream. Alternatively, make a lattice of cream so that the custard shows through and then pipe rosettes around the edge of the bowl. Top the rosettes with toasted almonds.

Gregory Usher

GREGORY USHER, the associate director of La Varenne, has a contagious enthusiasm for food. During demonstrations he can work for just so long before succumbing to temptation and dipping his finger into whatever is being prepared. Then you'll hear, "Mmmm. Isn't that good? It's what you would choose for a last meal!" And the next day he'll dive into something else, laugh at himself, and repeat, "Oh, there's nothing better! *This* would be the perfect last meal."

Ever since he was a freshman in high school, Gregory has known that cooking was for him. At the University of Oregon, where he majored in art history, he had a catering business on the side. When he switched locales to study at the Sorbonne, he formulated another goal—not only to cook, but to do it in Paris: "Food is loved and appreciated in France. Those who work with it are respected professionals. Meals are events. You need only walk down a street in Paris, any street, to see that the French live, eat, and think food."

Before coming to La Varenne in 1976, Gregory gained expertise working with *nouvelle-cuisine* stars, most importantly with Michel Guérard. At the school he manages both student and administrative affairs, while making an occasional tour to the U.S.A. He also somehow finds time to work on a guide to Paris restaurants.

An American who knows more about French cuisine than most Frenchmen, Gregory frequents the markets and restaurants of his adopted city and regales La Varenne students with reports of the best buys in the markets and of the dishes prepared by a newly discovered young chef.

Although he still dreams of opening his own restaurant in Paris —"A combined art gallery and restaurant would be ideal"—he is devoted to the idea of continuing his work at La Varenne: "We are to food what," he explains, "the Harvard Business School is to industry. As well as the mechanics, we teach the art."

Gregory Usher, in the upstairs kitchen, demonstrates how to hold the pan to turn out a perfect omelette.

Gregory Usher's Choices

Volcano Salad
(SALADE VOLCAN)

Salads such as this one that stress unusual combinations of colors and textures are called fantasy salads in France and are an important element of nouvelle cuisine. This is a recipe that Gregory learned while cooking at the Parisian club Régine's.

1 pound (500 g) thin green beans
salt and pepper
2 tomatoes, peeled, seeded, and chopped
3 ounces (90 g) large mushrooms
juice of ½ lemon
2 avocados
16–20 lettuce leaves
4 tablespoons cooked corn kernels

For the vinaigrette:
1 tablespoon mustard
2 tablespoons white-wine vinegar
6 tablespoons (95 ml) oil
salt and pepper
2 shallots, finely chopped

SERVES 4.

Cook the green beans in a large pan of boiling salted water 5–7 minutes or until barely tender. Drain, refresh under cold running water, and drain thoroughly.

For the vinaigrette: Whisk together the mustard and vinegar. Add the oil in a slow stream, whisking constantly to emulsify the dressing, and season to taste. Add the shallots to two thirds of the vinaigrette, leaving the remaining vinaigrette plain.

Mix the shallot vinaigrette into the green beans. Season the chopped tomatoes with salt and pepper and chill. Slice the mushrooms at the last minute and sprinkle with lemon juice to prevent them from darkening. Slice the avocados and sprinkle with lemon juice immediately.

On each plate arrange a bed of lettuce. Arrange the green beans in a mound in the center. Put overlapping avocado slices against one side of the mound and overlapping mushroom slices against the other side. Sprinkle the plain vinaigrette over the avocado and mushroom slices. Spoon a little tomato on top of the beans and sprinkle corn kernels over the tomato.

Creamed Leeks with Ham
(POIREAUX AU JAMBON À LA CRÈME)

Says Gregory, "This dish formed one of my first impressions of France, and to me it remains typical—a standard favorite in many French households."

> béchamel sauce (13) made with 3 cups (750 ml) milk, 1 slice of onion, 1 bay leaf, 8 peppercorns, 4 tablespoons (60 g) butter, 5 tablespoons (45 g) flour, salt and white pepper, and a pinch of grated nutmeg
> 8 medium leeks (about 1½ pounds or 750 g)
> salt and pepper
> 8 slices cooked ham
> ½ cup (50–60 g) grated Gruyère or Parmesan cheese

SERVES 8 as a first course or vegetable, or 4 as a main course.

Make the béchamel sauce (13). Cut the roots and most of the green tops from the leeks so they are about 6 inches (15 cm) long. Split them twice lengthwise down to but not through the white bulb and wash thoroughly. Cook them in boiling salted water 8–12 minutes or until tender, drain, refresh under cold running water, and drain again.

Let the leeks cool slightly, then roll each in a slice of ham, and arrange diagonally in a shallow buttered baking dish. Pour the sauce over them and sprinkle with the cheese. The leeks can be prepared 24 hours ahead and kept, covered, in the refrigerator.

To finish: Preheat the oven to 400°F (200°C). Bake the leeks 10–15 minutes or until very hot and browned.

Kipper Mousse
(MOUSSE DE HARENG FUMÉ)

This is an ideal make-ahead hors d'oeuvre for a cocktail party. For an amusing presentation, shape it into the form of a fish and decorate it with a caper eye and lemon-slice fins.

> ¾ pound (350 g) kipper fillets
> 1¼ cups (310 ml) milk
> ⅓ cup (80 g) unsalted butter, softened
> 2 tablespoons heavy cream
> pepper
> pinch of cayenne pepper
> squeeze of lemon juice
> salt—optional
> bread (for toasting)

SERVES 4.

Preheat the oven to 350°F (175°C). Bake the fillets in the milk in a covered dish 12–15 minutes or until they flake easily. Let cool to tepid, drain, and flake the meat. Discard the skin. Push the fish through a sieve to remove any bones.

In a blender, work half the kippers with half the butter and 1 tablespoon of the cream; then blend the remaining fish, butter, and cream. Alternatively, work the full amounts together in a food processor. Or, pound the fish in a mortar with a pestle and gradually work in the butter and cream.

Season the mousse to taste with pepper, cayenne pepper, lemon juice, and salt, if necessary. (NOTE: Kippers are often salty and more salt may not be needed.) Pile the mousse in a bowl or crock, cover, and chill. It can be made up to 48 hours before serving, but it should be left 2–3 hours at room temperature to soften. Serve with hot toast.

Gregory Usher

Fillets of Sole with Mushrooms and Tomatoes
(FILETS DE SOLE D'ANTIN)

This classic way of preparing sole, a preferred one at La Varenne, can be applied to any fine white fish. Try it with lemon sole or snapper.

3 pounds (1.5 kg) sole, yielding 1½ pounds (750 g) sole fillets
½ cup (125 ml) fish stock (6) made with 1 sliced onion, 1 table-
      spoon (15 g) butter, the heads and bones of the fish, 1 quart
      (1 L) water, 10 peppercorns, and a bouquet garni (1)
4 tablespoons (60 g) butter
2 shallots, finely chopped
½ pound (250 g) mushrooms, thinly sliced
2 tomatoes, peeled, seeded, and coarsely chopped
salt and white pepper
½ cup (125 ml) dry white wine
2 tablespoons (15 g) flour
¼ cup (60 ml) heavy cream
3 egg yolks
6 tablespoons (95 ml) water
1 tablespoon chopped parsley

SERVES 8 as a first course or 4 as a main course.

Skin and fillet the sole. Rinse and dry the fillets. Make the fish stock (6) and reduce to ½ cup (125 ml). Flatten the fillets by placing them between 2 pieces of waxed paper and pounding with the side of a heavy knife. Butter a sauté pan or flameproof casserole with 1 tablespoon (15 g) of the butter, sprinkle with the shallots, and add mushrooms and tomatoes. Season with salt and pepper. Fold the sole fillets in half, skin side inwards, and set them, tail end underneath, on the vegetables. Pour the fish stock and wine over the fish, cover with buttered foil, and simmer gently 7–10 minutes or until the fish just becomes opaque. Let cool slightly before lifting out the fillets and draining on paper towels. Transfer to a platter and keep warm. Pre-heat the broiler.

Boil the cooking liquid with the vegetables until reduced to about 1½ cups (375 ml). With a fork mash 2 tablespoons (30 g) of

139

the butter with the flour until smooth. Whisk in the butter and flour mixture piece by piece to thicken the sauce slightly. Simmer 2 minutes and then add the cream. In a small saucepan cook the egg yolks and water over low heat, whisking vigorously, until very frothy and slightly thickened. Whisk the yolks into the sauce. (NOTE: The yolks will curdle if overcooked, and the sauce cannot be reheated after the yolks are added.) Add the remaining tablespoon (15 g) of the butter in small pieces, shaking until incorporated, then add the parsley. Taste for seasoning and adjust if necessary. Spoon the sauce over the fish, brown very quickly under the broiler, and serve at once.

Brill or Turbot Bonne Femme
(BARBUE OU TURBOT BONNE FEMME)

This is a beautiful and traditional way of treating fine white fish— snapper, pompano, or gray sole, for example, are excellent cooked bonne femme. Fleurons, small crescents of puff pastry, are the classic garnish for any poached fish served in a rich sauce. Cut fleurons when- ever you have scraps of puff pastry, layer them with waxed paper, and freeze until needed.

3½–4 pounds (1.75 kg) brill or turbot
fish stock (6) made with 1 medium onion, 1 tablespoon (15 g) butter, the heads and bones of the fish, 1 quart (1 L) water, 10 peppercorns, a bouquet garni (1), 1 cup (250 ml) dry white wine
2 shallots, finely chopped
salt and pepper
1 tablespoon (15 g) butter
½ pound (250 g) mushrooms, thinly sliced
squeeze of lemon juice
puff-pastry crescents (fleurons)—for garnishing (optional)

For the sauce:
velouté sauce (**16**) made with the fish stock, 3 tablespoons (45 g)
    butter, 3 tablespoons (25 g) flour, salt and pepper
2 egg yolks
¼ cup (60 ml) heavy cream
2 tablespoons (30 g) butter
salt and pepper

Serves 6–8 as a first course or 4 as a main dish.

Fillet the fish and make the stock (**6**) with the bones. Cut the fillets into serving-size pieces if necessary. Skin, wash and dry the fillets and fold each piece in half. Butter a flameproof baking dish generously, sprinkle with the shallots, lay the fish on top, and season with salt and pepper.

Melt the butter in a pan, add the mushrooms, lemon juice, and salt and pepper. Cover with buttered waxed paper and cook over low heat 5 minutes or until the mushrooms are tender.

Pour enough fish stock over the fillets to cover, top with buttered waxed paper, and bring to a boil. Poach on top of the stove or in a moderate oven (350°F or 175°C) 5–6 minutes or until the fish just turns opaque. Drain the fillets well on paper towels, arrange them on a heatproof platter, and keep warm.

For the sauce: Strain the fish stock, add any that was not used to poach the fish, and reduce to 2 cups (500 ml). Make the velouté sauce (**16**) with the reduced stock and add the mushrooms with their liquid. Mix the egg yolks and cream in a bowl and stir in a little of the hot sauce. Stir this mixture back into the remaining sauce and heat gently, stirring, until it thickens slightly. (NOTE: Do not boil, or it will curdle.) Alternatively, for a lighter sauce, whisk the egg yolks with 1 table-spoon water over low heat until they thicken, as for hollandaise sauce (**20**). Add the thickened yolks directly to the hot sauce, then add the cream. Take the sauce from the heat and whisk in the 2 tablespoons (30 g) butter, piece by piece. Taste for seasoning and adjust if necessary.

Pour the sauce over the fish and brown briefly, just a few seconds, under a very hot broiler. Garnish the edge of the platter with puff-pastry crescents and serve immediately.

Chicken with Wine Vinegar
(POULET AU VINAIGRE DE VIN)

Though the amount of garlic in this recipe seems formidable, you will discover that the garlic flavor in the finished dish is surprisingly mild.

    3-pound (1.5 kg) roasting chicken, cut into 8 pieces
    salt and pepper
    6 tablespoons (95 g) butter
    15 garlic cloves, unpeeled
    1¾ cups (310 ml) wine vinegar
    2 ripe tomatoes, coarsely chopped
    1 tablespoon tomato paste
    bouquet garni (1)
    1 cup (250 ml) chicken stock (5)
    chervil or parsley sprigs (for decoration)

SERVES 4.

Season the pieces of chicken with salt and pepper. In a sauté pan heat 1 tablespoon (15 g) of the butter and add the pieces of chicken, skin side down, starting with the legs and thighs because they need the longest cooking. When they begin to brown, add the wing pieces and finally the breast pieces. When all are brown, turn them over and brown the other sides 1–2 minutes.

Add the garlic, cover, and cook over low heat 20 minutes. Pour off the excess fat. Add the vinegar and simmer about 10 minutes until well reduced. Add the tomatoes, tomato paste, and bouquet garni and simmer 10 minutes more. Transfer the pieces of chicken to a platter and keep warm. Add the stock to the pan and boil until very well reduced and concentrated in flavor. Taste for seasoning and strain, pressing hard on the garlic.

To finish: Reheat the sauce, remove from the heat, and whisk in the remaining butter in small pieces, a few at a time. Taste for seasoning and adjust if necessary. Pour the sauce over the chicken and decorate with a few sprigs of chervil or parsley.

Gregory Usher

Stuffed Chicken Grand-mère
(POULET FARCI GRAND-MÈRE)

A chicken filled with a pork stuffing and served with browned bacon, onions, and potatoes—this is the kind of simple home-style cooking Gregory likes so much.

3-pound (1.5 kg) chicken
2 tablespoons oil
3 tablespoons (45 g) butter
3 ounces (90 g) diced Canadian or other lean bacon
12 baby onions, blanched and peeled
3 large potatoes, peeled and cut into ½-inch (1.25 cm) cubes
salt and pepper

For the stuffing:
½ medium onion, finely chopped
1 tablespoon (15 g) butter
½ pound (250 g) ground pork
1 chicken liver, chopped
1 tablespoon chopped parsley
½ cup (70 g) fresh bread crumbs
salt and pepper

trussing needle and string

SERVES 4.

For the stuffing: Sauté the onion in the butter until lightly browned, add the pork, and stir to break up. Add the chicken liver and cook until it is just brown. Take from the heat, stir in the parsley and bread crumbs, and add salt and pepper to taste. Let cool, fill the chicken with the stuffing, and truss it.

In a casserole heat the oil and the 3 tablespoons butter, add the bacon and baby onions, and cook until brown. Remove the bacon and onions, add the potato cubes, and brown them. Take out the potatoes, put the chicken in the casserole, and brown it on all sides. Sprinkle with salt and pepper, cover tightly, and cook the chicken over very low heat, turning it from time to time, for 40 minutes, or

143

until it is almost tender. Return the onions, bacon, and potatoes to the casserole and season them with salt and pepper. Cover and continue cooking 5–10 minutes or until the chicken and vegetables are tender.

Remove the trussing strings, cut out and discard the backbone of the chicken, and cut the bird into quarters. Pile the stuffing on a platter or on plates and arrange the chicken quarters on top and the vegetable garnish around it.

Turkey Scallops with Cream
(ESCALOPES DE DINDE À LA CRÈME)

Thin slices of turkey breast can be treated much as veal scallops and given similar accompaniments. Buttered green noodles would be a colorful addition to this dish.

1½ pounds (750 g) turkey breast
½ cup (65 g) flour seasoned with ½ teaspoon salt and ¼ teaspoon pepper
4–5 tablespoons (60–80 g) butter, in all
¾ cup (185 ml) white wine
¾ cup (185 ml) chicken (5) or white veal (4) stock
½ pound (250 g) mushrooms, thinly sliced
½ cup (125 ml) heavy cream
salt and pepper
1 tablespoon chopped parsley

SERVES 4.

Cut the turkey breast diagonally into thin slices and flatten the slices to ¼ inch (6 mm) by pounding them between pieces of waxed paper with a rolling pin. Coat them with the seasoned flour, patting to remove the excess. In a sauté pan melt 3 tablespoons (45 g) of the butter and sauté several scallops over medium heat until browned,

144

allowing 2–3 minutes on each side. Arrange them overlapping on a platter or plates and keep warm. Sauté the remaining scallops in the same way, adding more butter if necessary.

Deglaze the pan with the wine and stock, add the mushrooms, and simmer until the sauce is slightly thickened. Add the cream, bring just to a boil, taste for seasoning, and adjust if necessary. Spoon the sauce over the scallops, sprinkle with the parsley, and serve.

Veal or Chicken Cutlets
(POJARSKI)

Because this Pojarski mixture has no starch or egg to bind the ground meat, handle it with care, especially when turning the "cutlets."

1½ pounds (750 g) lean veal or boned chicken breasts
salt and pepper
1½ cups (375 ml) heavy cream
flour (for shaping)
¼ pound (125 g) mushrooms, thinly sliced
4 tablespoons (60 g) butter
squeeze of lemon juice
2 tablespoons water
3 tablespoons brandy
½ cup (125 ml) dry white wine
1 tablespoon chopped parsley

SERVES 4.

Work the veal or chicken through the fine blade of a grinder once or twice until very finely ground. Beat it with a wooden spoon or with the dough hook of an electric mixer 3–4 minutes or until it leaves the sides of the bowl in a ball. Alternatively, work the meat in a food processor. (NOTE: This beating gives the Pojarski a light, smooth texture.) Add plenty of salt and pepper and beat in half the cream, 1 tablespoon at a time, beating well after each addition. If using a food processor, add the cream in a steady stream and stop beating as soon as it is mixed in. (NOTE: If overworked, the mixture tends to liquify.) Divide the meat into 4–6 portions and, on a lightly floured board, mold each into an oval about 1 inch (2.5 cm) thick.

Put the mushrooms in a pan with 1 tablespoon (15 g) of the butter, the lemon juice, 2 tablespoons water, and salt and pepper and cover first with buttered paper and then with a lid. Cook gently 3–4 minutes until tender. The mushrooms and cutlets can be prepared up to 6 hours ahead; keep them, covered, in the refrigerator.

To finish: In a skillet melt the remaining 3 tablespoons (45 g) of the butter and sauté the cutlets over medium heat 4–5 minutes on each side or until lightly browned. Add the brandy and flame. Transfer the cutlets to a platter or plates and keep warm while finishing the sauce. Add the wine to the skillet, simmer until well reduced, and add the mushrooms, their liquid, and the remaining cream. Bring just to a boil. Taste for seasoning and adjust if necessary. Spoon over the cutlets, sprinkle with the chopped parsley, and serve.

Pork Chops with Prunes
(CÔTES DE PORC AUX PRUNEAUX)

Prunes are used as a garnish in a number of French country dishes, especially with rabbit and pork. Marinating the pork tenderizes it and gives it more flavor.

four 1-inch-thick (2.5 cm) pork chops
3 cups (750 ml) tea—optional
½ pound (250 g) prunes
1 tablespoon oil

1 tablespoon (15 g) butter
2 tablespoons (20 g) flour
1 cup (250 ml) white wine
1 cup (250 ml) white veal (4) or chicken (5) stock
1 garlic clove, crushed
bouquet garni (1)
salt and pepper
1 tablespoon chopped parsley

For the marinade:
½ cup (125 ml) white wine
bouquet garni (1)
1 onion, coarsely chopped
1 carrot, coarsely chopped
6 peppercorns, slightly crushed
1 tablespoon oil

SERVES 4.

Combine marinade ingredients and marinate chops at room temperature, turning occasionally, for 4–12 hours or in the refrigerator 1–2 days. Pour boiling tea or water over the prunes, cover, and leave to soak about 3 hours.

Drain the pork, pat dry, and reserve the marinade and vegetables. In a sauté pan or shallow casserole heat the oil and butter and brown the chops on both sides. Remove the chops from the pan, add the onion and carrot from the marinade, and sauté lightly until they soften. Sprinkle the flour over the vegetables and cook, stirring, until well browned. Add the marinade and wine and bring to a boil. Add the stock, garlic, and bouquet garni and season with salt and pepper. Return the pork chops to the pan. Drain the prunes, add to the pan, cover, and simmer 35–45 minutes or until the chops are tender.

Transfer the chops to a platter or plates and top with the prunes. Strain the sauce. Reduce if necessary to a thin coating consistency, taste for seasoning, and spoon over the pork. Sprinkle with the parsley just before serving.

Braised Beef with Olives
(DAUBE ORLÉANAISE)

Gregory is very fond of country dishes, such as this daube, that simmer gently for hours. In contrast to the marinade in the preceding recipe for pork chops, here the marinade is cooked before being poured over the meat, so its flavor is more concentrated.

4–5 pounds (2 kg) round or chuck roast of beef
½ pound (250 g) salt pork, diced
⅓ cup (80 ml) rum
1 pound (500 g) tomatoes, peeled, seeded, and chopped
2 garlic cloves, crushed
2 tablespoons chopped fresh basil OR 1 teaspoon dried basil
salt and pepper
1 cup (200 g) pimiento-stuffed olives
1 tablespoon chopped fresh basil or parsley

For the marinade:
2 tablespoons olive oil
1 tablespoon wine vinegar
2 cups (500 ml) red wine
1 large onion, chopped
1 large carrot, chopped
bouquet garni (1)
strip of lemon zest
6 peppercorns

SERVES 6.

Bring all the ingredients for the marinade to a boil in a saucepan (not aluminum). Cool completely. Put the beef in a deep bowl and pour the marinade over it. Cover and refrigerate, turning the meat several times for 3 days.

Preheat the oven to 300°F (150°C). Remove the beef from the marinade and pat dry. Strain the marinade and reserve it and the vegetables. Blanch the salt pork by putting it in cold water, bringing to a boil, and simmering 5 minutes; drain and dry on a paper towel. In a deep heatproof casserole brown the salt pork, then remove it.

Brown the beef in the rendered fat over medium heat, remove it, and discard all but 1 tablespoon of the fat. Pat the reserved vegetables dry, add to the casserole, and cook over low heat 5–7 minutes until slightly soft. Return the beef to the casserole, add the rum, and flame. Add the salt pork, tomatoes, garlic, basil, salt and pepper, and strained marinade. Cover, bring to a boil, and braise in the preheated oven 3–4 hours or until meat is tender enough to cut with a spoon. The daube can be prepared up to 3 days ahead and kept in the refrigerator, or it can be frozen.

To finish: If necessary, reheat the daube in a 350°F (175°C) oven for an hour or until very hot. Transfer to a carving board and keep warm. Skim any fat from the sauce, add the olives, adjust seasoning if necessary, and bring back just to a boil. Carve beef and arrange on a platter or plates. Spoon a little sauce over the meat and sprinkle with basil or parsley. Serve the remaining sauce separately.

Beef Stew with Walnuts
(RAGOÛT DE BOEUF AUX NOIX)

With this, as with all brown stews, be sure to color the pieces of meat a few at a time over high heat. Otherwise their juices will escape and the meat will steam instead of browning.

4 tablespoons oil
1½–2 pounds (750 g–1 kg) beef chuck, cut into 2-inch (5 cm) cubes
2 onions, sliced
1 carrot, sliced
1 stalk celery, sliced
2 garlic cloves, crushed

3 tablespoons (25 g) flour
1 cup (250 ml) red wine
2 cups (500 ml) brown veal (2) or brown beef (3) stock
bouquet garni (1)
salt and pepper

For the garnish:
zest of 1 orange, cut into needle-like strips
½ head of celery, cut into ½-inch (1.25 cm) slices
2 tablespoons (30 g) butter
salt
¾ cup (90 g) walnut halves

SERVES 4.

In a heavy-bottomed casserole heat the oil and brown the beef cubes a few at a time. Remove them and add the onions, carrot, and celery. Cook slowly, stirring occasionally, until soft but not brown. Add the garlic and cook 1–2 minutes more. Add the flour and cook, stirring, until the roux is a rich brown. Add the wine, stock, bouquet garni, and salt and pepper. Return the meat to the casserole and bring the stew to a boil. Cover and simmer on top of the stove or in a preheated 350°F (175°C) oven 2–2½ hours or until very tender. If the sauce is not thick, remove the lid during the last half hour of cooking to reduce it. Transfer the beef to another pan and strain the sauce over it. The meat can be cooked up to 3 days ahead. Cool and keep, covered, in the refrigerator or freeze.

To finish: Put the orange zest in cold water, bring to a boil, and boil 3–4 minutes. Refresh under cold running water and drain thoroughly. Cook the celery slowly in the butter, stirring occasionally, for 5–7 minutes or until soft but not brown. Sprinkle with salt, add the walnuts, and mix well. Reheat the stew if necessary, taste for seasoning, and spoon it into a serving dish or onto plates. Top with the celery-and-walnut mixture and the orange zest and serve.

Lamb Ragoût
(RAGOÛT D'AGNEAU)

This lamb stew is made with as many fresh vegetables as possible. In winter you may be reduced to using potatoes, carrots, and onions, and the meat may be mutton, but in spring make it with baby lamb and new vegetables.

1½ pounds (750 g) boned shoulder or breast of lamb, cut into 1½-inch (4 cm) pieces
salt and pepper
2 tablespoons oil
12–16 baby onions
2 tablespoons (15 g) flour
1 tablespoon tomato paste
1 garlic clove, crushed
bouquet garni (1)
2–2½ cups (500–625 ml) brown veal (2) or brown beef (3) stock
1 teaspoon arrowroot mixed to a paste with 1 tablespoon water—optional
2 tomatoes, peeled, seeded, and chopped
8 baby carrots, peeled, OR 2 large carrots, peeled and quartered
1 turnip, peeled, cut into 8 pieces
1½ pounds (750 g) small new potatoes, peeled, OR 3–4 large potatoes, peeled and quartered
1 cup (150 g) shelled fresh peas OR ⅓ pound (150 g) frozen peas
2 tablespoons chopped parsley

SERVES 4.

Preheat the oven to 425°F (220°C). Season the lamb with salt and pepper. In a casserole heat the oil and brown the lamb on all sides, a few pieces at a time. Take them out, add the onions, and brown them. Remove them, return the meat to the casserole, and sprinkle it with flour. Cook 5 minutes in the preheated oven or until the flour is browned. Remove the casserole from the oven, let cool slightly, and add the tomato paste, garlic, bouquet garni, and enough stock to cover the meat. Cover and simmer 1 hour. Transfer the meat

151

to another casserole, skim any fat from the sauce, and strain the sauce over the meat. If necessary, thicken it to a light coating consistency by stirring the arrowroot paste into the boiling liquid and heating gently.

Add the tomatoes and carrots to the casserole, more stock to cover the meat if necessary, cover, and continue simmering 30 minutes. Add the onions, turnip, and potatoes and simmer 10 minutes longer. The meat and vegetables should all still be slightly firm. The ragoût can be prepared up to 48 hours ahead and kept, covered, in the refrigerator.

To finish: If necessary reheat the ragoût on top of the stove or in the oven. Meanwhile, blanch the fresh peas in boiling water 2 minutes, refresh in cold running water, and drain thoroughly. Add the peas to the stew and continue cooking 20 minutes or until the lamb is tender. If using frozen peas, add them 8–10 minutes before the end of cooking. Taste for seasoning and adjust if necessary. Ladle the ragoût into a serving bowl or onto plates, sprinkle with parsley, and serve very hot.

Parisienne Potatoes
(POMMES PARISIENNE)

Since realizing, toward the end of the 18th century, that potatoes were fit for human consumption, the French have done marvelous things with them. The preparation below is an important garnish in many classic French meat dishes.

4–5 large potatoes (about 2 pounds or 1 kg), peeled
1 tablespoon oil
3 tablespoons (45 g) butter
salt and pepper

¾–1-inch (2–2.5 cm) ball cutter

SERVES 4.

Use the cutter to cut the potatoes in balls. To make the frying easier and quicker, you may blanch them: Cover with cold water, bring to a boil, drain, and dry well.

In a skillet or frying pan heat the oil and butter, add the potato balls, and sauté 10–15 minutes until tender, shaking the pan from time to time so they brown evenly. Start over high heat to sear the outside and then lower the heat to cook them through. The potatoes can be cooked 15–20 minutes ahead and kept warm in a low oven. Sprinkle with salt and pepper just before serving.

Artichoke Bottoms à la Niçoise
(FONDS D'ARTICHAUTS À LA NIÇOISE)

The French refer to preparing artichoke bottoms for cooking as "turning" them. Turn the artichoke with one hand and cut off the leaves with the other.

salt
1 lemon
4 artichokes
4 tablespoons (25 g) dry bread crumbs
2 tablespoons oil

   For the filling:
stewed tomato pulp (**19**) made with 2 tablespoons oil, ½ onion,
   2 pounds (1 kg) tomatoes, 1 garlic clove, a bouquet garni (**1**),
   and salt and pepper
4 anchovy fillets, diced

SERVES 4.

Bring a large pan of water to a boil. Add salt and squeeze in the juice of ½ lemon; keep the lemon to rub the turned artichokes.

To prepare the artichoke bottoms: Add the juice of the other ½ lemon to a bowl of cold water. Break off the stem from the first artichoke. Using a very sharp knife and holding it against the side of the artichoke, cut off all the large bottom leaves, leaving a soft cone of small leaves in the center. Trim this cone level with the top of the artichoke base. Rub the base well with the cut lemon to prevent discoloration. Trim the base to an even round shape, slightly flattened on the bottom. Rub again with cut lemon and drop the artichoke into the bowl of cold lemon water. When all are prepared, drain them, drop into the boiling water, and simmer 15–20 minutes or until tender. Drain and scoop out the chokes with a teaspoon.

For the filling: Make the stewed tomato pulp (19), adding 1 garlic clove, chopped, with the tomatoes. Cook until very thick, remove from the heat, and stir in the diced anchovies. The artichokes can be prepared 24 hours ahead and kept, covered, in the refrigerator.

To finish: Preheat the oven to 425°F (220°C). Pile the tomato filling into the artichoke bottoms and put them in a shallow buttered baking dish. Sprinkle with bread crumbs and the oil. Bake in the pre-heated oven about 15 minutes or until hot, then brown briefly under the broiler.

Potatoes in Cream
(POMMES DE TERRE À LA CRÈME)

French crème fraîche, *with its slightly acid taste, gives an excellent flavor to this dish. Try the recipe for it* (41).

> 4 medium potatoes (1½ pounds or 750 g) small new potatoes, unpeeled
> 1½ cups (375 ml) heavy cream
> salt and pepper
> pinch of grated nutmeg

SERVES 4.

Put the potatoes in cold salted water to cover, top with lid, and bring to a boil. Simmer 15–20 minutes or until just tender, drain, and peel. Cut large potatoes in 1-inch (2.5 cm) chunks but leave small potatoes whole. The potatoes can be prepared 6–8 hours ahead; keep them at room temperature.

To finish: Put the potatoes in a pan and pour the cream, seasoned with salt and pepper and nutmeg, over them. Simmer the potatoes, uncovered, over very low heat 10–12 minutes or until the cream has thickened to a sauce.

Oranges with Caramel
(ORANGES AU CARAMEL)

The crisp caramel topping for these oranges dissolves rather quickly once exposed to moisture, so it should be added at the last moment. You may wish to sprinkle only a small amount of crushed caramel over each orange and pass the rest separately.

8 large seedless oranges
1 tablespoon Grand Marnier

For the poaching syrup:
½ cup (100 g) sugar
2 cups (500 ml) water
1 tablespoon Grand Marnier

For the caramel:
1½ cups (300 g) sugar
1 cup (250 ml) cold water
½ cup (125 ml) warm water

SERVES 4.

For the poaching syrup: Bring the sugar, water, and 1 tablespoon of Grand Marnier to a boil. Pare the zest from the 8 oranges and cut it in needle-like shreds with a sharp knife. Blanch the zest in boiling water 3–4 minutes, refresh with cold running water, and drain. Add the blanched zest to the syrup and poach 10–15 minutes or until it is tender and the syrup is thick.

Meanwhile, with a serrated or very sharp knife, cut away all the white pith and the inner membranes from all the oranges. Hold the oranges over a bowl while peeling to catch the juice and add it to the syrup. Cut the oranges crosswise into ¼-inch (6 mm) slices, re-constitute each orange, and spear the slices with a toothpick to hold them together. Pile in a glass bowl or set in dishes.

For the caramel: Oil a baking sheet. In a heavy-bottomed sauce-pan heat the sugar and cold water until dissolved, then boil steadily without stirring until it is a deep golden caramel color. Remove from heat and, when the bubbles have subsided, pour half the caramel onto the prepared baking sheet. Add the warm water to the remaining caramel in the pan; stand back because it will sputter. Bring back to a boil, stirring to dissolve the caramel, and add the zest and syrup. Let cool, then put a heaping tablespoon of orange zest on each orange, pour the sauce around the oranges, sprinkle them with 1 tablespoon Grand Marnier, and chill. When the caramel on the baking sheet is cold and hard, crush it with a rolling pin, in a mortar with a pestle, or in a food processor. Keep in an airtight container. Keep the oranges, covered, in the refrigerator. They can be prepared up to 1 day ahead.

Just before serving, sprinkle the oranges with crushed caramel.

Gregory Usher

Light Apple Tart
(TARTE AUX POMMES LÉGÈRE)

This modern version of a traditional favorite should be almost as thin as a crêpe. Bake it in as hot an oven as possible so that the pastry and apples cook and the sugar caramelizes, all at the same time.

4 Golden Delicious apples, peeled, halved, and cored
3 tablespoons (45 g) butter, cold
¼ cup (50 g) sugar

For the light pie pastry:
1¼ cups (160 g) flour
7 tablespoons (110 g) unsalted butter
1 teaspoon salt
2–4 tablespoons cold water

10-inch (25 cm) pie or tart pan

SERVES 6.

For the pie pastry: Sift the flour onto a working surface and make a large well in the center. Pound the 7 tablespoons (110 g) butter with a rolling pin to soften it slightly. Put butter, salt, and 2 tablespoons of the water in the well and work together with your fingertips until partly mixed. Gradually work in the flour, pulling the dough into large crumbs. If the crumbs are dry, add up to 2 tablespoons more water, a little at a time. Using a dough scraper, cut the dough to mix. When the dough is nearly smooth, work it lightly on the working surface by pushing it away with the heel of your hand and gathering it up with the dough scraper until it is pliable. (NOTE: Because of the high proportion of butter, you must be especially careful not to over-work this dough.) Press the dough into a ball, wrap, and chill at least 30 minutes.

Preheat the oven to 475°F (245°C). Roll out the dough to a very thin round (about ⅟₁₆ inch or 1.5 mm thick) and line the bottom, but not the sides, of the pan. Unlike most pie pastry, the dough should be stretched instead of being slid gently into the pan. Prick the dough with a fork.

157

Cut the apples into very thin slices and arrange them in one layer on the dough, rounded sides out and in concentric circles. (NOTE: To prevent burning, overlap the apple slices slightly so the dough is completely covered.) Cut the 3 tablespoons (45 g) butter into thin pieces. Sprinkle the apples with the sugar and arrange the pieces of butter on top at approximately equal intervals. Bake in the preheated oven 10–15 minutes or until the apples are tender and the sugar is caramelized. Serve hot. The tart can be baked ahead and reheated in a hot oven.

Maurice Ferré

IMAGINE a block of ice a foot and a half wide and a yard high. A handsome, gray-haired man with courtly manners steps up to it and attacks with a hammer, a chisel, and a saw. Twenty minutes later, the chunk is a graceful swan ready to glide to the table carrying assorted *sorbets* on its back. The sculptor is Maurice Ferré, chef *pâtissier* of Maxim's, who explains, "When I came to Maxim's twenty-five years ago, ice vases were traditional in the restaurant, and I just thought I'd expand the idea."

Chef Ferré gives various accounts of his beginning on the path to Maxim's. He says, "When I was young I was a *petit gourmand* and ate a lot of cake. Cakes were expensive, so I wanted to make them myself." Or he'll tell you that he had a friend who was an apprentice *cuisinier*. "He didn't have to go to school, and he moved away from our small village and lived alone in the city. He wore these really nice pants [the blue-and-white checked pants worn by all chefs and apprentices in France], and all the girls ran after him. I wanted to be just like him." There wasn't an opening for a cuisine apprentice at the time, but he found one in pastry and at fifteen began his career. His first employer promised that, after a stint in *pâtisserie*, there would be an opening in cuisine, but by the time the opportunity came, Ferré was enamored of pastry and has stayed so ever since.

Chef Ferré started at Maxim's when he was twenty and over the years has delighted celebrities there from Rex Harrison to Rod Stewart to Henry Kissinger with his appetizers, desserts, and *petits fours*. He hasn't been at Maxim's famous kitchen continuously; he interrupted his work to do military service for two years and to spend four years

159

in America helping to start Maxim's in Chicago. It was there that he developed a fondness for Americans and for cheeseburgers, in that order.

Now, as an associate chef at La Varenne, he has added teaching to his schedule. Everyone at La Varenne who attends even one of his classes is grateful that chance launched the 15-year-old Maurice Ferré on the road to *pâtisserie*, for he can teach with consummate skill how to make the pastries and candies that are his specialties. The admiration is mutual, in part, as he points out to American students, because he has "only the best memories of the United States."

Maurice Ferré,
Chef Pâtissier of Maxim's,
sifts flour for a pastry
class in the downstairs
practical kitchen

Maurice Ferré's Choices

Mushroom Bouchées
(BOUCHÉES AUX CHAMPIGNONS)

Roll and shape puff pastry as quickly as possible so the butter won't melt.

> puff pastry (27) made with ¾ pound (350 g) unsalted butter, 2 cups (260 g) all-purpose flour, 1 cup (120 g) cake flour, 1½ teaspoons salt, 1½ teaspoons lemon juice, and ¾–1 cup (185–250 ml) ice water
> 1 egg, beaten with ½ teaspoon salt (for glaze)
>
> *For the filling:*
> béchamel sauce (13) made with 2 cups (500 ml) milk, 1 slice of onion, 1 bay leaf, 6 peppercorns, salt and pepper, a pinch of grated nutmeg, 3 tablespoons (45 g) butter, and ⅓ cup (45 g) flour
> ¾ pound (350 g) mushrooms, quartered or diced
> juice of ½ lemon
> salt and pepper
> 3 egg yolks
> ½ cup (125 ml) heavy cream
>
> *3½-inch (9 cm) fluted round cookie cutter*
> *2½-inch (6 cm) fluted or plain round cookie cutter*

SERVES 8.

Make the puff pastry (27) and chill. Roll the dough to less than ¼ inch (6 mm) thick and stamp out 16 rounds with the larger cutter. Transfer 8 rounds to a baking sheet sprinkled with water. Brush with egg glaze, taking care that it does not drip onto the sheet. With the smaller cutter, cut a circle from the center of each of the remaining rounds. (NOTE: These circles are not needed for the bouchées. Reserve for another use.) Turn the rings over and set them on top of the rounds on the baking sheet. Press gently to seal. Brush the rings with glaze and chill 15 minutes.

Preheat the oven to 425°F (220°C). Bake the bouchées 15–20 minutes or until puffed and brown. If not serving immediately, transfer to a rack to cool; while the bouchées are still warm, cut around the inside edge and carefully lift out the circle of crisp pastry in the center. Scoop out any uncooked dough. The bouchées can be kept 1–2 days in an airtight container, or they can be frozen.

For the filling: Make the béchamel sauce (**13**). Put the mushrooms in a saucepan with lemon juice, salt and pepper, and a spoonful or two of water. Cover and cook over high heat 4–5 minutes or until the liquid boils up to the top of the pan. Add the mushrooms and their liquid to the béchamel.

Reheat the bouchées if necessary in a preheated 250°F (120°C) oven. To finish the filling: Reheat it if cool. Mix the yolks and cream in a bowl, stir in a little of the hot sauce, and stir this mixture back into remaining sauce. Heat until it thickens slightly but do not boil. Taste for seasoning and adjust if necessary. If not served immediately, keep hot in a water bath. Just before serving, fill each bouchée with some of the mushroom mixture, mounding it well, and top each one with the circle of pastry taken from the center of the bouchée.

Asparagus in Puff Pastry
(FEUILLETÉES AUX ASPERGES, SAUCE HOLLANDAISE)

This recipe shows that Chef Ferré keeps abreast of new ideas in French cooking though he doesn't eschew the old. Light vegetable first courses are all the rage. And the nouvelle-cuisine chefs favor rectangular puff-pastry cases to round shells because they're quicker to cut and waste less dough.

> puff pastry (**27**) made with ½ pound (250 g) unsalted butter, 1⅓ cups (175 g) all-purpose flour, ⅔ cup (80 g) cake flour, 1 teaspoon salt, 1 teaspoon lemon juice, and ½–¾ cup (125– 185 ml) cold water
> 1 egg, beaten with ½ teaspoon salt (for glaze)
> 3 pounds (1.5 kg) asparagus

hollandaise sauce (20) made with ½ pound (250 g) butter, 4 tablespoons water, 4 egg yolks, salt and white pepper, and juice of ½ lemon

SERVES 6.

Make the puff pastry (27) and chill. Roll out the dough to ¼ inch (6 mm) thick and cut six 4- × 5-inch (10 × 13 cm) rectangles. Put the rectangles on a baking sheet sprinkled with water, brush with egg glaze, and refrigerate for 15 minutes. Preheat the oven to 475°F (245°C). Bake the pastry 5 minutes in the very hot oven, then turn the heat down to 400°F (200°C), and continue baking about 10 minutes or until the rectangles are puffed and browned. If not serving immediately, transfer to a rack to cool. While still warm, cut each in half horizontally and scoop out any uncooked dough. The pastry cases can be kept 1–2 days in an airtight container, or they can be frozen.

Prepare the asparagus by cutting off and discarding the ends so that all the stalks are 5 inches (12.5 cm) long. Peel the stalks and keep in a bowl of plain water.

Make the hollandaise sauce (20) and keep warm over hot water. Reheat the pastry cases in a preheated 250°F (120°C) oven if necessary.

Drop the asparagus into boiling salted water and boil 10 minutes or until just tender. Drain well. Arrange the bottom halves of the pastry rectangles on a platter or on individual plates, top with the asparagus, the sauce, and finally with the pastry lids set slightly askew to expose the filling. Serve immediately.

Leek Tart

(TARTE AUX POIREAUX)

This would normally be a first course in France, but if you line the pie shell with a layer of ham before adding the leeks, it can be served as a main dish for luncheon or supper.

pie pastry **(24)** made with 1½ cups (195 g) flour, 6 tablespoons (95 g) butter, 1 egg yolk, ½ teaspoon salt, and 4–5 table-spoons water
2 pounds (1 kg) leeks
5 ounces (150 g) butter
¾ cup (185 ml) water
salt and pepper
béchamel sauce **(13)** made with 1 cup (250 ml) milk, 1 slice of onion, 1 bay leaf, 6 peppercorns, salt and pepper, a pinch of grated nutmeg, 2 tablespoons (30 g) butter, and 2 table-spoons (15 g) flour
2 egg yolks

9–10 inch (23–25 cm) tart or pie pan

SERVES 6 as a first course.

Make the pie pastry (24) and chill. Butter the tart pan. Roll out the pastry to just under ¼ inch (6 mm) thick and line the pan. Prick the dough lightly with a fork and chill ½ hour or until firm. Pre-heat the oven to 400°F (200°C).

Cut the roots and the green tops from the leeks, wash the bulbs thoroughly, and cut into ½-inch (1.25 cm) slices. In a saucepan heat the butter and water over low heat until the butter melts. Add the leeks, cover, and cook 8–10 minutes or until just tender. Season to taste.

Line the tart shell with foil, fill with dried beans or rice, and bake in the hot oven 10–12 minutes until the pastry is set and begin-ning to brown. Remove the beans and foil and bake the shell 8–10 minutes more or until lightly browned. Remove from the oven and let the shell cool slightly. Reduce the oven to 350°F (175°C).

Make the béchamel sauce (13). Take from the heat. Stir a few spoonsful of the hot sauce into the egg yolks and then stir this mixture into the rest of the sauce. Add the cooked leeks and their liquid and adjust the seasoning to taste.

Fill the pastry with the leek and béchamel-sauce mixture and bake 20 minutes or until hot. Serve at once.

Scrambled Eggs and Salmon in Pastry Shells
(CROUSTADES D'OEUFS BROUILLÉS AU SAUMON FUMÉ)

The French take scrambled eggs seriously and cook them carefully over very low heat until thickened but not firmly set. They are an ideal stretcher for an expensive ingredient such as smoked salmon.

> pie pastry (**24**) made with 1½ cups (195 g) flour, 6 tablespoons (95 g) butter, 1 egg yolk, ½ teaspoon salt, and 4–5 tablespoons cold water
> ½ pound (250 g) smoked salmon
> 12 eggs
> salt and pepper
> ¼ pound (125 g) butter
> few sprigs parsley (for garnish)
>
> *six 4-inch (10 cm) tartlet pans*

SERVES 6.

Make the pie pastry (**24**) and chill. Butter the tartlet pans and group them close together. Roll out the dough to just under ¼ inch (6 mm) thick. Wrap it loosely around the rolling pin and then unroll over the pans. Press the pastry into the pans with a ball of dough dipped in flour and roll the pin across the pans to cut off excess dough. Prick the shells with a fork and chill until firm. Preheat the oven to 400°F (200°C).

Line the tartlet shells with rounds of foil and fill with dried beans or rice, or put a smaller tartlet pan inside each. Set them on a baking sheet and bake in the preheated oven 8–10 minutes or until the pastry is set and lightly browned. Remove the beans and foil and return the shells to the oven 5–7 minutes or until crisp and brown. Let cool slightly and then remove from the pans. The shells can be made up to 48 hours ahead and kept in an airtight container.

To finish: Reheat the tartlet shells if necessary in a low oven. Chop all the salmon except one slice; cut this into 12 thin strips. With a whisk or fork beat the eggs with salt and pepper until thoroughly mixed and slightly frothy. Melt the butter in a heavy-bottomed saucepan, add the eggs, and cook over very low heat, stirring constantly with a wooden spoon, for 3–5 minutes or until the eggs are the consistency of a thick sauce with some small soft curds. Add the chopped salmon, remove from the heat, and spoon the eggs into the pastry shells. Garnish each with 2 strips of salmon and a tiny sprig of parsley. Serve immediately.

Sardine Turnovers
(CHAUSSONS AUX SARDINES)

Apples are the most common filling for chaussons in France, but Chef Ferré uses the idea for these novel turnovers stuffed with sardines.

    puff pastry (**27**) made with ½ pound (250 g) butter, 1⅓ cups (175 g) all-purpose flour, ⅔ cup (80 g) cake flour, 1 teaspoon salt, 1 teaspoon lemon juice, and ½–¾ cup (125–185 ml) water
8 ounces (250 g) canned boneless sardines, drained
1 egg, beaten with ½ teaspoon salt (for glaze)

    For the anchovy butter:
8 anchovy fillets
½ cup (125 ml) milk
¼ pound (125 g) butter, softened
pepper

5-inch (13 cm) fluted round pastry cutter

MAKES 10 turnovers.
    Make the puff pastry (**27**) and chill.
    For the anchovy butter: Soak the anchovy fillets in the milk to remove excess salt; leave 10 minutes and drain. Crush the anchovies in a mortar with a pestle and work in the butter with pepper to taste. Alternatively, make the anchovy butter in a blender or food processor.

Shape the butter into a cylinder 1 inch (2.5 cm) in diameter, wrap in waxed paper, and chill until firm.

Preheat the oven to 425°F (220°C) and sprinkle a baking sheet with water. Roll out the pastry dough approximately $\frac{1}{16}$ inch (1.5 mm) thick and stamp out 5-inch (13 cm) rounds. With a pastry brush dipped in water, moisten the border of each round. Set a sardine in the center of each, fold the pastry in half, and crimp the edges closed. Put the turnovers on the prepared baking sheet and chill at least 15 minutes.

Brush the tops with egg glaze, being careful not to get any on the edges, and bake in the preheated oven 15–20 minutes or until the pastry is puffed and browned. Arrange the pastries on a platter or on plates. Slice the anchovy butter into rounds and set one on each hot turnover just before serving.

Orange Tartlets
(TARTELETTES À L'ORANGE)

Since the oranges in this tart are not peeled, try to get very thin-skinned ones. The slight bitterness of the peel that remains after the orange slices are poached in sugar syrup makes them an ideal topping for the sweet pastry cream.

> 4 medium oranges
> sweet pie pastry (25) made with 1½ cups (195 g) flour, ½ teaspoon salt, ½ cup (100 g) sugar, 4 egg yolks, 1 teaspoon vanilla extract, and ¼ pound (125 g) butter
> pastry cream (34) made with 6 egg yolks, ½ cup (100 g) sugar, 5 tablespoons (45 g) flour, and 2 cups (500 ml) milk
> Chantilly cream (36) made with ⅓ cup (80 ml) heavy cream, and 1 teaspoon sugar
> sugar (for caramelizing)

For the sugar syrup:
2 cups (400 g) sugar
2 cups (500 ml) water

eight 4-inch (10 cm) tartlet pans

SERVES 8.

For the sugar syrup: Heat the sugar and water over low heat until dissolved and then boil 2–3 minutes or until the syrup is clear. Cut 3 of the unpeeled oranges evenly into very thin slices (about ⅛ inch or 3 mm); discard any seeds. Put them into the syrup, bring to a boil, reduce the heat, and poach 20 minutes or until the peel is tender. Remove from the heat and leave to macerate. Squeeze the juice from the remaining orange and set aside.

Make the sweet pie pastry (25) and refrigerate. Preheat the oven to 400°F (200°C). Roll out the pastry dough and line the pans. Prick the bases with a fork and chill ½ hour or until firm. Line the dough with foil, fill with dried beans or rice, and bake 10–12 minutes until the pastry is set and beginning to brown. Remove the beans and foil and bake the shells 7–10 minutes longer or until lightly browned. Remove from the oven and let the shells cool.

Meanwhile, prepare the pastry cream (34). While the cream is still warm, add the orange juice and then leave to cool.

Drain the orange slices well and chop about ⅓ cup (40 g) of them, using any less than perfect slices. Make the Chantilly cream and fold it and the chopped oranges into the pastry cream. Spread the cream evenly over the bottom of the tartlet shells.

Overlap 3 orange slices on top of each cream-filled tartlet. Sift a heavy coating of sugar evenly over the tartlets and caramelize under the broiler. Cool before serving. The tartlets are best eaten within 3–4 hours.

Tangerine Tart
(TARTE AUX CLÉMENTINES)

Clementines are a type of tangerine from Italy, Spain, and Israel that have become a great favorite in France.

sweet pie pastry (**25**) made with 1 cup (130 g) flour, ⅓ teaspoon salt, ⅓ cup (65 g) sugar, 3 egg yolks, ¾ teaspoon vanilla extract, and 5 tablespoons (80 g) unsalted butter
2 tablespoons Grand Marnier
pastry cream (**34**) made with 3 egg yolks, 4 tablespoons (50 g) sugar, 2½ tablespoons (25 g) flour, and 1 cup (250 ml) milk
5 fresh tangerines or 1 can mandarin oranges in light syrup
½ cup (125 ml) apricot glaze (**38**)

For the frangipane:
5 tablespoons (80 g) butter, softened
½ cup (100 g) sugar
1 egg, beaten to mix
1 egg yolk
2 teaspoons Grand Marnier
¾ cup (110 g) blanched almonds, ground
2 tablespoons (15 g) flour

9–10 inch (23–25 cm) tart or pie pan

SERVES 6.

Make the sweet pie pastry (**25**) and refrigerate. Butter the tart pan. Roll out the chilled pastry to just under ¼ inch (6 mm) thick and line the pan. Prick the dough lightly with a fork and chill ½ hour or until firm. Preheat the oven to 400°F (200°C).

For the frangipane: Cream the butter, gradually beat in the sugar, and continue beating until light and soft. Gradually add the egg and the extra yolk, beating well after each addition. Add the 2 teaspoons Grand Marnier and then stir in the ground almonds and flour. (NOTE: Do not beat the mixture now or the oil will be drawn out of the almonds.)

Spoon the frangipane into the pastry shell. Bake in the preheated oven 25–30 minutes or until the frangipane is set and brown; reduce heat to 350°F (175°C) if the pastry browns too quickly. Remove the tart from the oven and sprinkle it at once with 1 tablespoon of the Grand Marnier. Leave it to cool. Make apricot glaze (38).

Make the pastry cream (34), flavoring it with the remaining tablespoon of Grand Marnier, and spread it on top of the frangipane.

Peel and section fresh tangerines, or thoroughly drain canned mandarin orange sections. Arrange the tangerine sections on the pastry cream in a flower pattern and brush them with the melted apricot glaze. The tart is best eaten the day it is baked.

Orange Cake
(CAKE À L'ORANGE)

French pastry cooks use the English word to refer to simple, unfrosted cakes like this "cake à l'orange," reserving the French "gâteau" for their more elaborate creations.

> 5 ounces (150 g) crystallized orange peel, chopped
> ⅓ cup (80 ml) Grand Marnier
> 6 ounces (180 g) butter, softened
> 1¼ cups (170 g) powdered sugar
> 1 tablespoon (20 g) corn syrup
> 4 eggs
> grated zest of ½ orange
> 2 cups (260 g) flour
> 2 teaspoons (7 g) baking powder
>
> *deep 9-inch (23 cm) round cake pan*

SERVES 6.

Macerate the crystallized peel in ¼ cup (60 ml) of the Grand Marnier.

In a mixing bowl beat the butter, powdered sugar, and the corn syrup until thick and light. Beat in the eggs one by one. If the mixture begins to separate, warm the bowl over boiling water. Mix in the macerated peel, drained, and the grated orange zest. Sift the flour with the baking powder, then fold it into the egg batter in 2–3 batches. Let rest at room temperature 20 minutes. Preheat the oven to 350°F (175°C). Butter the cake pan generously and flour it.

Gently pour the batter into the pan—it should be about ¾ full— and smooth the top with a spatula. Bake 1 hour or until a toothpick inserted in the middle of the cake comes out clean. Remove the cake from the pan, set on a rack to cool, and sprinkle with the remaining Grand Marnier. The cake improves in flavor if it is kept for several days, well-wrapped in aluminum foil.

Orange Chanteclaire
(CHANTECLAIRE À L'ORANGE)

As his choice of recipes shows, Chef Ferré loves citrus fruits, especially oranges. Recipes like this one may make you a devotee, too.

2 whole medium oranges
sugar syrup (37) made with ½ cup (100 g) sugar, ½ cup (125 ml) water, and ½ tablespoon Grand Marnier
sponge cake (30) made with ¾ cup (95 g) flour, a pinch of salt, 4 separated eggs, ¾ cup (150 g) sugar, and ½ teaspoon vanilla extract
¼ ounce (7 g) gelatin
¼ cup (60 ml) water
custard sauce (35) made with 1 cup (250 ml) milk, 5 egg yolks, ½ cup (100 g) sugar, and the zest of 2 additional oranges, cut into strips
juice of the 2 oranges
Chantilly cream (36) made with 1 cup (250 ml) heavy cream and 1 tablespoon (12 g) sugar

powdered sugar (for sprinkling)

¼ cup apricot glaze (**38**) made with ¼ cup (75 g) apricot preserves and 1 tablespoon (12 g) sugar

9-inch (23 cm) round cake pan

Serves 6.

Cut the 2 unpeeled oranges into even ¼-inch (6 mm) slices.
Make sugar syrup (**37**), but wait to flavor it with the Grand Marnier
until the oranges have been cooked. Simmer the orange slices in the
syrup for 10 minutes, then add the Grand Marnier, and leave to
macerate.

Make the sponge cake (**30**) and cool.

Sprinkle the gelatin over the water and leave for 5 minutes or
until spongy. Make the custard sauce (**35**), adding the strips of orange
zest to the milk as it heats and removing them from the finished sauce.
Add the gelatin to the hot custard sauce, stirring well so it dissolves
completely. Leave to cool, stirring occasionally. Squeeze the juice
from the 2 oranges and make the Chantilly cream.

Cut the cake horizontally into 2 layers. Drain the syrup from the
cooked orange slices and use it to moisten both layers of the cake.
Wipe out the cake pan and dust it with a generous coating of powdered sugar, then line the bottom and sides with the macerated orange
slices. Chill.

When the custard mixture is cool, set it over a bowl of ice water.
Stir the mixture as it cools. When it is cold to the touch and you feel
it becoming thicker, it is beginning to set. Now gently fold in the
Chantilly cream and orange juice. Pour half of this mixture into the
lined cake pan and top with one layer of the cake, browned side
down. Pour the remaining custard over the cake, set the second layer
on top, browned side up, and press lightly. Refrigerate at least 5 hours
or overnight.

To finish: Melt the apricot glaze (**38**) over low heat. Unmold
the gâteau: First put the bottom of the cake pan in hot water for 10
seconds, then turn the cake out onto a serving plate. Brush the surface
of orange slices with glaze. The cake can be served immediately or
kept in the refrigerator for up to 6 hours.

Grapefruit Alhambra
(ALHAMBRA AU PAMPLEMOUSSE)

When a student tasted this cake after a recent demonstration, she breathed, "It was worth the whole trip just for this."

> sponge cake (**30**) made with ¾ cup (95 g) flour, a pinch of salt, 4 eggs, and ¾ cup (150 g) sugar
>
> ½ cup (150 g) apricot jam or orange marmalade
>
> Chantilly cream (**36**) made with 2 cups (200 ml) heavy cream and ¼ cup (50 g) sugar
>
> ¼ ounce (7 g) gelatin
>
> ½ cup (125 ml) fresh grapefruit juice
>
> apricot glaze (**38**) made with ½ cup (150 g) apricot preserves and 2 tablespoons (25 g) sugar
>
> *9-inch (23 cm) round cake pan*
>
> *11- × 16-inch (28 × 40 cm) baking sheet*

SERVES 6.

Butter the cake pan and the baking sheet, line them with waxed paper, and butter the paper. Make the cake batter (**30**), gently pour one quarter of it into the cake pan, and spread the remaining batter over the baking sheet. Bake the cakes 12–15 minutes or until they just begin to shrink from the sides of the pans. Turn them out onto racks and spread the large cake, while still warm, with the jam or marmalade. Roll it up, from a short end, like a jelly roll and cut the roll into slices ¼ inch (6 mm) thick. Clean and butter the cake pan and line it with the slices of cake.

Make the Chantilly cream. Sprinkle the gelatin over ¼ cup (60 ml) of the grapefruit juice and leave for 5 minutes or until spongy. Heat the remaining juice, add the gelatin mixture, stirring to dissolve, then set aside to cool. When cool, fold into the Chantilly cream and pour the mixture into the lined cake pan. Chill thoroughly. When the cream filling is quite cold, place the round layer of cake on top and press down lightly.

To finish: Melt the apricot glaze (**38**). Unmold the cake onto a serving plate and brush with the glaze.

Maurice Ferré

Chocolate Alexandra
(ALEXANDRA AU CHOCOLAT)

Besides its rich chocolate flavor, this gâteau has a delightful contrast in textures between delicate, creamy mousse and sweet, crunchy meringue.

> Swiss meringue (**40**) made with 8 egg whites, 2½ cups (500 g)
>   sugar, and ½ cup (75 g) unsweetened cocoa
> powdered sugar (for dusting)
>
> *For the mousse:*
> ½ pound (250 g) semisweet chocolate
> ¼ pound (125 g) butter, softened
> 3 egg yolks
> 6 egg whites
> ¼ cup (50 g) sugar
>
> *pastry bag with ½-inch (1.25 cm) plain tip*

SERVES 8–10.

Preheat the oven to 200°F (100°C). Lightly grease and flour 2 baking sheets. Sift 2 cups (400 g) of the sugar with the cocoa. Make the Swiss meringue (**40**), beating in ½ cup (100 g) of the sugar as soon as the whites are stiff and folding in the cocoa-sugar mixture as usual after another minute of beating. Pipe three 7-inch (18 cm) rounds onto the prepared baking sheets. With any remaining meringue, pipe fingers ½ inch (1 cm) wide to be used to decorate the cake. Cook in the very slow oven 3 hours or until crisp. Remove and let cool in a dry place. The meringues can be kept in an airtight container for up to 1 week.

For the mousse: Melt the chocolate over hot water. Remove from heat and gradually beat in the butter to make a smooth cream. Beat the egg yolks and add them, mixing well; the heat of the chocolate should cook and thicken them slightly. Beat the egg whites until stiff, gradually adding the ¼ cup (50 g) sugar. Stir one third of the whites into the chocolate mixture, blending well. Gently fold in the rest of the whites.

To finish: Spread the top of each meringue round with a thick layer of the chocolate mousse, stacking the rounds to form a 3-layer cake. Coat top and sides with the remaining mousse. Chill 1 hour, then break any meringue fingers you have into 1½-inch (4 cm) pieces, and sprinkle them on the sides and top of the gâteau. The cake can be kept, refrigerated, up to 3 days. Just before serving, sprinkle lightly with powdered sugar.

Pear Sherbet

(SORBET AUX POIRES)

Though many sherbet recipes call for extra water and for egg whites, Chef Ferré makes his with fruit purée and sugar syrup, which allows the full flavor of the fruit to come through clearly.

> 3 pounds (1.5 kg) ripe pears
> juice of 4 lemons
> 1 vanilla bean OR 1 teaspoon vanilla extract

> *For the sugar syrup:*
> 2 pounds (1 kg) syrup
> 2 quarts (2 L) water
> juice of 2 lemons

MAKES about 1½ quarts (1.5 L).

Peel, core, and quarter the pears. Drop them into cold water acidulated with half the first quantity of lemon juice and set aside.

For the sugar syrup: Heat the sugar, water, and juice of 2 lemons over low heat until dissolved, then boil 2–3 minutes or until the syrup is clear.

Add the pear quarters, drained, and the vanilla bean to the syrup. Bring to a boil, cover, and reduce heat. Poach 10 minutes or until the pears are soft. Remove from the heat, add the vanilla extract if you did not use a vanilla bean, and let the pears cool in the syrup.

Remove the pears and purée them in a food processor, blender, or food mill. Strain the syrup. Measure the pear purée, combine it with an equal volume of the syrup, and add the remaining lemon juice. Pour the mixture into an ice-cream freezer and churn until set.

Nectarine Sherbet
(SORBET AUX NECTARINES)

Peaches can be substituted for the nectarines in this recipe. A garnish of fresh raspberries or strawberries makes a beautiful color contrast, or serve the sherbet with raspberry sauce (see Peaches Cardinal, p. 57).

3 pounds (1.5 kg) ripe nectarines
1 vanilla bean OR 1 teaspoon vanilla extract
juice of ½ lemon

For the sugar syrup:
1½ pounds (750 g) sugar
1½ quarts (1.5 L) water

MAKES about 1½ quarts (1.5 L).

Peel, pit, and quarter the nectarines.

To make the sugar syrup: Heat the sugar and water over low heat until dissolved, then boil 2–3 minutes or until the syrup is clear.

Add the nectarines and vanilla bean to the syrup. Bring to a boil, cover, and reduce heat. Poach 5–10 minutes or until the nectarines are quite soft. Remove from the heat, add the vanilla extract if you did not use a vanilla bean, and let the nectarines cool in the syrup.

Remove the nectarines and purée in a food processor, blender, or food mill. Strain the syrup. Measure the nectarine purée, combine it with an equal volume of the syrup, and add the lemon juice. Pour the mixture into an ice-cream freezer and churn until set.

Sultanas
(SULTANES)

At Maxim's and other fine restaurants in France, petits fours or small candies like the ones below are served at the end of the meal with coffee. It's a custom worthy of emulation, especially when they're your own hand-dipped chocolates.

> 2 cups (300 g) whole blanched almonds
> ½ cup (100 g) sugar
> 1 egg white
> praline (39) made with ½ cup (75 g) whole unblanched almonds
> and 6 tablespoons (80 g) sugar
> ½ cup (125 ml) heavy cream
> powdered sugar (for dusting)
> 5 ounces (150 g) semisweet chocolate, chopped
> 3 tablespoons (45 g) butter
> 1½ tablespoons oil

MAKES 25–30 sultanas.

In a food processor or blender grind 1 cup (150 g) of the first quantity of blanched almonds with the sugar. Add the egg white a little at a time and continue to process or blend until the almonds have been reduced to a firm paste. Remove almond paste and set aside. Wash and dry the container of your machine. Reserve 30 whole almonds and grind the rest to a fine powder in the processor or blender. Make the praline (39).

In a saucepan bring the cream to a boil. Remove from heat and mix in the almond paste, almond powder, and praline. Turn out onto a working surface liberally sprinkled with powdered sugar and leave to cool. With your hands, roll 1 scant tablespoon at a time of the mixture into a flat oval, dusting with powdered sugar to prevent sticking. Leave the ovals to dry overnight.

Melt the chocolate with the butter and oil over hot water, stirring, until just warm to the touch. Maintaining the heat at this temperature, hold each almond oval over the pan on a fork or a slotted spatula and spoon the chocolate over it to coat it. Set on a sheet of aluminum foil and leave for an hour or until set, but before the chocolate has set, garnish the top of each candy with a whole almond. Once set, they can be transferred to a cool, dry place to harden overnight. Sultanas can be kept, refrigerated, for 4–5 days.

Pistaches
(PISTACHES)

In France, couverture, a chocolate with a high percentage of cocoa butter, is used to coat candies. If you can get it, try substituting it for the chocolate, butter, and oil combination in this and the preceding recipe.

    1 cup (150 g) whole blanched almonds
    ½ cup (100 g) sugar
    1 egg white
    ½ cup (75 g) blanched and peeled pistachio nuts
    2 tablespoons kirsch
    3 tablespoons (25 g) powdered sugar
    powdered sugar (for dusting)
    5 ounces (150 g) semisweet chocolate, chopped
    3 tablespoons (45 g) butter
    1½ tablespoons oil

MAKES 25–30 candies.

    In a food processor or blender grind the almonds with the sugar. Add the egg white a little at a time and continue to process or blend until the almonds have been reduced to a firm paste. Remove almond paste and set aside. Wash and dry the container of your machine. Reserve 30 pistachios and chop the rest in the processor or blender. Stir the chopped nuts into the almond paste along with the kirsch and the 3 tablespoons powdered sugar. Turn out the mixture onto a work surface liberally sprinkled with powdered sugar. With your hands, roll 1 teaspoon at a time of the mixture into a flat round, dusting with powdered sugar to prevent sticking. Leave the rounds to dry overnight.

Melt the chocolate with the butter and oil over hot water, stirring, until just warm to the touch. Maintaining the heat at this temperature, hold each round over the pan on a fork or a slotted spatula and spoon the chocolate over it to coat it. Set on a sheet of aluminum foil and leave for an hour or until set, but before the chocolate has set, garnish the top of each candy with a pistachio. Once set, they can be transferred to a cool, dry place to harden overnight. The candies can be kept, refrigerated, for 4–5 days.

Léon Zelechowski

"I'M ALWAYS curious to know other things," says Chef Léon Zelechowski. This might well be the motto for his life, which has already included much change, experience, and learning, though he's only in his early thirties. It seems that even before he was born he was destined to flourish in new climes. His father and uncle emigrated from Russia. At one point the two had a sharp, hour-long debate over the merits of going to America versus those of settling in France. "In that hour," says Léon, "it was decided whether I would be French or American."

Léon is one of nine children. "Food is very important in a large family, you know, because you always have to fight for it." Perhaps because of this, he chose cooking early as a career. Between thirteen and sixteen, Léon apprenticed in an Auvergne restaurant. He worked from seven-thirty in the morning until one o'clock the next morning, was off only on Sunday evening after four o'clock, and never saw the sun during the winter. He passed his CAP exams (*certificat d'aptitude professionnelle*) in cuisine and then worked in a deluxe restaurant in the spa town of Vichy where, he laughs as he recounts, he served elaborate lobster dishes every day to people taking health cures.

Now executive chef for one of the top French maritime companies, Chef Léon has taught at a professional school in a château in Burgundy for a year and a half, has been chef for both the Austrian and Belgian embassies in Paris, and has cooked in Canada. He says that the Austrians wanted hearty meat-and-potato meals, whereas the Belgians expected a cuisine replete with rich cream and butter sauces. In Canada the requests were for grilled meat and salad. Before Chef Léon returned to France, his employer asked that he leave behind five liters of his excellent vinaigrette dressing. As to his present clientele, Léon says, the French are the most demanding of all.

For one year, Chef Léon concentrated on pastry rather than cuisine, and, at the end of that time, he passed the exams for a CAP in *pâtisserie*. It's unusual for a chef to be highly skilled in both areas and rare for one to hold a *certificat* in each.

"Cooking is exacting," says Léon. "To know your profession, you must use your skills constantly and always challenge yourself." Léon continues to do so. He is working full-time as a chef, teaching as an associate chef at La Varenne, and thinking of opening his own restaurant, perhaps in North America. He enjoys teaching almost as much as learning and comments, "La Varenne students are so particularly good to work with because they really want to learn."

Léon Zelechowski,
"turning" vegetables
in the practical kitchen

Léon Zelechowski's Choices

FIRST COURSES

Tomato and Bean Soup, p. 184
Deviled Sardines, p. 185
Egg Croquettes, p. 185
Pork Terrine, p. 187

MAIN COURSES

Baked Sea Bream with Oranges and Limes, p. 188
Monkfish of the Emerald Coast, p. 189
Chicken Breasts with Port, p. 191
Chicken Suprêmes Archduke, p. 192
Braised Ham with Madeira Sauce, p. 194
Braised Leg of Lamb, p. 195

VEGETABLES

Lenten Spinach, p. 196
Creamed Carrots, p. 197
Stuffed Tomatoes, p. 198
Eggplant Italienne, p. 199

DESSERTS

Strawberry Charlotte Malakoff, p. 200
Caramel-glazed Puffs, p. 202
Crêpes Creole, p. 203

Tomato and Bean Soup
(SOUPE AUX TOMATES ET AUX HARICOTS SECS)

A simple, well-flavored bean soup that is always welcome.

2 cups (400 g) dried white beans
1½ quarts (1.5 L) water
bouquet garni (1)
1 tablespoon olive oil
1 medium onion, chopped
2 strips bacon, chopped
3 medium tomatoes, peeled, seeded, and chopped
1 garlic clove
salt and pepper
1 tablespoon chopped parsley

SERVES 4.

Rinse the beans under running water and soak 2 hours in cold water. Drain. Bring 1½ quarts (1.5 L) water to a boil and add the beans. Reduce the heat to a simmer, add the bouquet garni, and cover the pot.

In a saucepan heat the olive olive and sauté the onion and bacon until lightly browned. Add the tomatoes and garlic. Cook this mixture over moderate heat 5 minutes, stirring often. Add to the beans and continue simmering them, covered, for 1½ hours or until beans are soft. Add salt halfway through the cooking time.

Remove the bouquet garni and purée the soup in a blender, food processor, or food mill. The soup should be somewhat thick, but if necesary thin it with a little water. Add pepper, taste, and adjust the seasoning if necessary. (NOTE: The bacon may have already made the soup salty enough.) The soup can be made ahead and kept in the refrigerator up to 3 days. To serve, ladle the soup into bowls and sprinkle with chopped parsley.

Léon Zelechowski

Deviled Sardines

(SARDINES À LA DIABLE)

The waters around Sardinia are particularly rich in sardines, hence the name. These good, inexpensive little fish are excellent prepared simply, as below.

¾ pound (350 g) canned skinless sardines, packed in oil
¼ teaspoon cayenne pepper
2 tablespoons Dijon mustard
¼ cup (30 g) flour
1 egg, beaten to mix
1 cup (100 g) dry bread crumbs
oil (for frying)
1 tablespoon chopped parsley

SERVES 4–6.

Drain the sardines and put on paper towels to absorb the remaining oil. Blend the cayenne pepper with the mustard and coat the sardines on all sides, being careful not to tear the flesh. Roll in the flour, dip in the egg, and then roll in the bread crumbs. Heat the oil to 350°F (175°C) and fry until golden, just about 20–30 seconds. Drain on paper towels. Sprinkle with parsley and serve.

Egg Croquettes

(OEUFS EN CROQUETTES)

Most croquettes are made like these, so small pieces of nearly any meat, fish, vegetable, or cheese can be added to the thick sauce instead of the hard-cooked eggs.

½ pound (250 g) mushrooms
thick allemande sauce (17) made with 1 cup (250 ml) velouté

185

sauce (**16**), the mushroom stems, 1 egg yolk, salt and pepper,
a squeeze of lemon juice, and grated nutmeg
1 tablespoon oil
1 tablespoon (15 g) butter
salt and pepper
8 hard-cooked eggs, finely chopped
1 truffle, finely chopped—optional
deep fat (for frying)

For the coating:
2 eggs beaten with 1 tablespoon oil and 1 tablespoon water
1 cup (100 g) bread crumbs
1 cup (130 g) flour

SERVES 4–6.

Stem the mushrooms and chop the stems. Make the allemande sauce (**17**), adding the chopped stems.

Dice the mushroom caps. Heat the oil and the butter in a skillet, add the mushrooms, and salt and pepper and sauté over high heat, tossing often, for 3–4 minutes or until browned. Leave to cool.

Mix the hard-cooked eggs with the mushrooms and the truffle and stir in the allemande sauce. Taste for seasoning and adjust if necessary. Put the croquette mixture in a buttered tray and rub the top with butter to prevent a skin from forming. Chill about 2 hours or until very firm.

To coat the croquettes: Prepare 2 trays, one containing the beaten eggs and the other the bread crumbs. Roll half the croquette mixture on a well-floured working surface, shaping it into a long cylinder about 1 inch (2.5 cm) in diameter. Cut into 3-inch (7.5 cm) pieces. Transfer the pieces carefully to the tray containing the eggs and roll them to coat, then roll them in the bread crumbs. (NOTE: Be sure the ends are well coated.) Transfer the croquettes to a plate or baking sheet (they must not touch each other) and chill, uncovered, for 30 minutes or up to 6 hours.

To finish: Heat the deep fat to 360°F (180°C) and fry the croquettes, a few at a time, for 2–3 minutes until golden brown. (NOTE: Do not overcook or they will burst.) Keep them hot in a warm oven with the door ajar while frying the remaining croquettes. Serve at once.

Léon Zelechowski

Pork Terrine

(TERRINE DE PORC)

Like all terrines, this one benefits from being made at least two days before serving to allow the flavors to mellow.

½ pound (250 g) sliced barding fat or bacon
1 tablespoon (15 g) butter
1½ onions, chopped
1½ pounds (750 g) pork (half fat, half lean), ground
½ pound (250 g) pork liver, finely chopped
2 garlic cloves, finely chopped
big pinch ground ginger
big pinch ground cloves
big pinch grated nutmeg
2 eggs, beaten to mix
2 tablespoons Calvados or applejack
salt and pepper
1 bay leaf
1 branch thyme

   To seal the terrine:
2–3 tablespoons water
⅓ cup (45 g) flour

1½-quart (1.5 L) terrine or casserole with tight-fitting lid

SERVES 8.

Line the terrine or casserole with the barding fat or bacon, reserving a few slices for the top. Preheat the oven to 350°F (175°C).

Melt the butter in a small pan and sauté the onions until soft but not brown. Mix the onions with the pork and the liver, the garlic, ginger, cloves, nutmeg, eggs, Calvados, and plenty of salt and pepper. Beat with a wooden spoon to thoroughly distribute the seasonings. Sauté a small piece and taste for seasoning—it should taste quite spicy.

Fill the lined terrine with the mixture and lay the reserved barding fat or bacon on top. Set the bay leaf and branch of thyme on top of the bacon and cover with the lid.

187

To seal the terrine: In a cup or bowl lightly stir the water into the flour to make a paste. (NOTE: Do not beat the paste or it will become elastic.) Seal the gap between mold and lid with the paste.

Set the terrine in a water bath, bring the water to a boil on top of the stove, and then cook in the heated oven 1¼–1½ hours or until a skewer inserted into the mixture through the hole in the terrine lid for 30 seconds is hot to the touch when withdrawn. (NOTE: Regulate the heat so the water keeps simmering; if much of it evaporates, add more.) Cool until tepid. Remove the flour paste and the lid and press the terrine with a board or plate and a 2-pound (1 kg) weight until cold.

Keep the terrine in the refrigerator for at least 2 days or up to 1 week before serving. To serve, unmold the terrine, cut part of it into thick slices, and arrange them on a platter or on plates. Or, serve the terrine directly from the mold.

Baked Sea Bream with Oranges and Limes
(DORADE À L'ORANGE ET AU CITRON VERT)

You will find that sea bream is often called porgy in our markets and may not be large enough for this recipe. Red Snapper, mullet, or bass can also be used to make this nouvelle-cuisine dish.

stewed tomato pulp (**19**) made with 2 tablespoons oil, ½ onion, finely chopped, 2 pounds (1 kg) tomatoes, a small bouquet garni (**1**) and salt and pepper
2 oranges
4 limes
5–6 pound (2.25–2.75 kg) whole sea bream, scaled and cleaned, but with head left on if possible
salt and pepper
½ cup (125 ml) dry white wine
½ cup (125 ml) water

SERVES 4.

Make the stewed tomato pulp (**19**). Preheat the oven to 350°F (175°C).

Peel the zest from ½ orange and 2 of the limes and cut into needle-like shreds. Blanch the zest by putting it in a pan of cold water, bringing to a boil, and boiling it 5 minutes. Refresh under cold running water and drain thoroughly. Stir the zest into the well-reduced stewed tomato pulp and adjust seasoning if necessary. The mixture can be prepared up to 2 days ahead and kept, covered, in the refrigerator.

Wash the fish, cut off the fins, and trim the tail to a "V." Season with salt and pepper. Put the fish in a buttered baking dish or roasting pan and add the wine and water. Score the top deeply with diagonal slashes 2 inches (5 cm) apart so the fish will cook evenly. Spoon the tomato mixture over it. Cut the 2 unpeeled limes into thin slices and arrange them overlapping down the back of the fish. Bake the fish in the heated oven 35–40 minutes or until the flesh just turns opaque; make a small slit with a knife and check to see that it is opaque down to the bone.

Meawnhile, cut the white skin from the 2 oranges and cut the sections from the membrane. To serve, transfer the fish to a platter and garnish it with the orange sections.

Monkfish of the Emerald Coast
(LOTTE CÔTE D'ÉMERAUDE)

Other shellfish besides the mussels and clams that are called for in this recipe can be used to garnish the monkfish. Scallops, for instance, simmered for 2–3 minutes in the court bouillon, would be a good addition.

court bouillon (**7**) made with 1½ quarts (1.5 L) water, 1 carrot, and 1 onion, both sliced, a bouquet garni (**1**), 6 peppercorns, a pinch of salt, and 2 cups (500 ml) white wine

3 pounds (1.5 kg) mussels, clams, or preferably a mixture of both
2 pounds (1 kg) monkfish (angler fish), in one piece
¼ cup (60 g) butter
5 tablespoons (45 g) flour
½ cup (1.25 ml) heavy cream
2 tablespoons (30 g) capers
2 lemons, sliced

SERVES 4.

Make the court bouillon (7) and strain into a wide pot. Scrub the mussels thoroughly under cold running water and remove the beards. Discard any with broken shells or any open ones that do not close when tapped. Wash the clams several times.

Remove skin from both sides of the fish. Put the fish into the court bouillon and, if necessary, add more water to just cover. Bring just to a boil, cover, and poach over low heat about 20 minutes or until a skewer inserted in the fish for 30 seconds is hot to the touch when withdrawn. Drain, reserving the court bouillon. Transfer the fish to a platter and keep warm.

Cook the mussels and the clams separately, each in ½ cup (1.25 ml) of the reserved cooking liquid. Cook them in a covered pot over high heat, tossing occasionally, for 3–4 minutes or just until the shells open. Shell them. Reserve their cooking liquids and let stand for a few minutes so all the sand falls to the bottom. Pour most of the 2 liquids carefully into a measuring cup, leaving the sandy liquid in the bottom of the pans. Add enough court bouillon to the measured liquid to make 3 cups (750 ml).

Melt the butter, whisk in the flour, and cook over low heat until foaming but not browned. Whisk in the measured liquid, bring to a boil, and simmer 2–3 minutes. Stir in the cream, the mussels and clams, and heat briefly. Taste for seasoning and adjust if necessary. Coat the fish with the sauce and shellfish, sprinkle with the capers, and decorate with the lemon slices.

Léon Zelechowski

Chicken Breasts with Port
(SUPRÊMES DE VOLAILLE AU PORTO)

*A suprême is the boneless breast from one side of a chicken. The first
wing bone may be cut off or left attached.*

> basic brown sauce (**9**) made with 1 cup (250 ml) well-flavored
>   brown veal stock (**2**), 2 teaspoons arrowroot or potato starch,
>   1 tablespoon cold water, salt and pepper
> 4 suprêmes (boned breasts of 2 chickens)
> salt and pepper
> ⅓ cup (45 g) flour
> 6 tablespoons (95 g) butter
> ¼ cup (60 ml) port wine

SERVES 4.

Make the basic brown sauce (**9**). About 20 minutes before
serving, season the suprêmes with salt and pepper and coat with flour,
patting off the excess. Heat 4 tablespoons (60 g) of the butter and fry
the suprêmes 5–6 minutes on each side until golden brown and tender.
Keep warm until ready to serve.

Discard the fat from the pan, add the port and brown sauce, and
bring to a boil, stirring to deglaze the pan juices. Strain the sauce,
bring it back to a boil, adjust seasoning if necessary and, off the heat,
whisk in the remaining butter in small pieces. (NOTE: Do not reheat
the sauce now or it will separate.) Arrange the chicken suprêmes on
a platter or on plates, spoon some sauce over each, and serve the rest
separately.

Chicken Suprêmes Archduke
(SUPRÊMES DE VOLAILLE ARCHIDUC)

Suprêmes of chicken lend themselves to many variations. This one, with its red-hued paprika sauce and green, spinach-flavored potatoes, is particularly attractive.

> 6 suprêmes (boned breasts of 3 chickens)
> salt and pepper
> pinch of sweet Hungarian paprika
> 2 tablespoons (30 g) butter
>
> *For the sauce:*
> 5 tablespoons (80 g) butter
> 1 onion, chopped
> 2 teaspoons paprika
> 2 tablespoons (15 g) flour
> ⅓ cup (80 ml) white wine
> 1¼ cups (310 ml) chicken stock (**5**)
> ⅓ cup (80 ml) heavy cream
> salt and pepper
>
> *For the spinach-flavored duchesse potatoes:*
> 1 pound (500 g) spinach
> salt and pepper
> 4 tablespoons (60 g) butter, in all
> 4–5 medium potatoes (2 pounds or 1 kg), peeled
> pinch of grated nutmeg
> 3 egg yolks
>
> *pastry bag with medium star tip*

SERVES 6.

For the paprika sauce: Melt 2 tablespoons (30 g) of the butter, add the onion, and cook slowly, stirring occasionally, for 5–7 minutes or until soft but not brown. Whisk in the paprika and flour and cook, whisking, for 1–2 minutes or until bubbling. Remove from the heat, whisk in the wine, and bring to a boil. Add the stock and simmer 20 minutes, adding the cream a little at a time. Taste for seasoning and adjust if necessary. Strain through a fine sieve. The sauce can be made up to a day ahead and kept, covered, in the refrigerator.

For the spinach-flavored duchesse potatoes: Remove the stems from the spinach and wash the leaves. Blanch in a large pan of boiling salted water 2–3 minutes or until just tender. Refresh under cold running water. Squeeze out as much water as possible. Purée in a food mill, blender, or food processor. Heat 1 tablespoon (15 g) of the butter, add the spinach, and heat, stirring, until dry.

Cut each potato in 2–3 pieces, put in cold salted water, bring to a boil, and simmer 15–20 minutes or until tender. Preheat the oven to 425°F (220°C); butter a baking sheet. Drain the potatoes and push them through a sieve. Return to the saucepan and beat in the remaining 3 tablespoons (45 g) of butter, salt and pepper, and nutmeg. Continue beating over low heat until light and fluffy. Take from the heat and beat in the egg yolks. Beat in the spinach purée, taste for seasoning, and adjust if necessary. While the mixture is still warm, with the pastry bag pipe it onto the baking sheet in 6 oval nests a little larger than the suprêmes. Bake in the oven 15 minutes or until set and arrange on a platter or on plates.

Meanwhile, season the suprêmes with salt and pepper and paprika. Heat the 2 tablespoons (30 g) butter in a sauté pan, add the suprêmes, and cook over low heat 3–5 minutes on each side or until just tender. Put one suprême in each potato nest.

Bring the sauce to a boil, remove from the heat, and stir in the remaining butter in small pieces. Coat the suprêmes with sauce and serve the remaining sauce separately.

Braised Ham with Madeira Sauce
(JAMBON BRAISÉ, SAUCE MADÈRE)

The cooking time in this recipe depends on the type of ham used. Country ham must be soaked in cold water and then simmered before braising, but precooked ham needs no prior preparation.

> 3–4 pound (1.5–1.75 kg) butt or shank of country or precooked ham
> 1 tablespoon oil
> 1 tablespoon (15 g) butter
> 2 carrots, diced
> 2 onions, diced
> 1 stalk celery, sliced
> ¼ cup (60 ml) Madeira
> 1 cup (250 ml) brown beef stock (3)
> bouquet garni (1)
> pepper
> Madeira sauce (11) made with 2 cups (500 ml) basic brown sauce (9), ⅓ cup (80 ml) Madeira, salt and pepper

SERVES 4.

If using country ham heavily cured with salt, soak it 12 hours in cold water. Put the ham in a pan with fresh water to cover. Top with a lid, simmer 1 hour, and drain.

Preheat the oven to 325°F (165°C). In a casserole heat the oil and butter and cook the vegetables, covered, for 5–7 minutes until they are soft and the fat is absorbed. Put the ham on top, pour the Madeira over it, and flame. Add the stock, bouquet garni, and pepper. Cover and braise in the heated oven 1½ hours or until the ham is very tender. The ham can be braised up to 48 hours ahead and reheated. Keep it, covered, in the refrigerator.

Make the Madeira sauce (11).

To finish: Reheat the ham and the Madeira sauce if necessary. Transfer the ham to a carving board and keep in a warm place 10 minutes. Then carve the ham and arrange the slices on a platter or on plates. Spoon a little sauce over the slices to coat them and serve the remaining sauce separately.

Léon Zelechowski

Braised Leg of Lamb
(GIGOT D'AGNEAU BRAISÉ)

If you're not fond of rare leg of lamb, try braising it as in this recipe. You'll have well-done meat that is still juicy and tender.

1 garlic clove—optional
5–6 pound (2.25–2.75 kg) leg of lamb
3 tablespoons oil
2 onions, sliced
2 carrots, sliced
2 stalks celery, sliced
1½ cups (375 ml) dry white wine
2 cups (500 ml) brown veal stock (2)
bouquet garni (1)
sprig of fresh rosemary OR 1 teaspoon dried rosemary
salt and pepper
bunch watercress

SERVES 6–8.

Make 3–4 slits in the lamb with a small, pointed knife. Cut slivers from the garlic cloves and insert them into the slits. The garlic may be omitted if you prefer. In a large deep heatproof casserole heat the oil and brown the lamb on all sides. Add the onions, carrots, and celery, lower the heat, and continue cooking gently until the vegetables are lightly browned. Preheat the oven to 350°F (175°C). Crush the remaining garlic and add it to the vegetables with the wine, stock, bouquet garni, rosemary, and salt and pepper. Cover, bring to a boil, and braise in the preheated oven 2½–2¾ hours or until the lamb is very tender. The lamb can be cooked up to 48 hours ahead and kept, covered, in the refrigerator.

To finish: If necessary, reheat the lamb in a preheated 350°F (175°C) oven about 45 minutes or until very hot. Transfer it to a platter or carving board and keep hot. Strain the cooking liquid, skim off any fat, and boil if necessary until well flavored and reduced to about 1 cup (250 ml). Taste for seasoning and adjust if necessary.

195

The lamb can be carved in the kitchen and then reconstituted on the bone, or it can be carved at the table. Garnish the platter with the watercress, spoon a little sauce over the meat before serving, and serve the remaining sauce separately.

Lenten Spinach
(ÉPINARDS AU MAIGRE)

Maigre, which means lean, certainly does not refer to the slimming properties of this butter and cream-rich dish, but rather to its appropriateness for the "lean" times of religious fasts. It is a delicious addition to meals all year round.

> 3 pounds (1.5 kg) fresh spinach
> salt and pepper
> 5 tablespoons (80 g) butter
> pinch of sugar
> ¼ teaspoon grated nutmeg
> 1 cup (250 ml) heavy cream
>
> *For the croûtons:*
> 6 slices firm, white bread, cut in half diagonally, crusts removed
> 3 tablespoons oil and 3 tablespoons (45 g) butter (for frying)

SERVES 4.

Remove the stems from the spinach and wash the leaves well in 3 changes of cold water. Cook the spinach, uncovered, in boiling salted water 5 minutes or until tender. (NOTE: Avoid using an aluminum pan because it will discolor the spinach.) Drain, then refresh the spinach under cold running water. Squeeze it by handfuls to remove as much water as possible, then chop the leaves.

For the croûtons: Fry the bread in the butter and oil until golden brown on both sides and drain on paper towels.

In a saucepan melt 4 tablespoons (60 g) of the butter. Add the spinach and cook, stirring, about 5 minutes to remove any remaining moisture. Season with the sugar, nutmeg, and salt and pepper. Add the cream. Cook the spinach slowly, stirring often, for 10 minutes, and then taste for seasoning. The spinach and croûtons can be prepared a few hours ahead. Before serving, reheat spinach and croûtons if necessary. Dot the spinach with the remaining butter and garnish with the croûtons.

Creamed Carrots
(CAROTTES À LA CRÈME)

Léon points out that this carrot recipe is good any time of year since it can be adjusted to suit the seasonal carrots. The baby carrots of springtime can be cooked whole, while medium ones are best treated as in the recipe. For old carrots, try the French trick of quartering them lengthwise and removing the woody interior.

1 pound (500 g) carrots, peeled and sliced
¼ pound (125 g) butter
pinch of salt
2 tablespoons (25 g) sugar
medium béchamel sauce (13) made with 1 cup (250 ml) milk,
    1 slice of onion, 1 small bay leaf, 6 peppercorns, 1½ table-
    spoons (20 g) butter, 1½ tablespoons (12 g) flour, salt and
    white pepper, and grated nutmeg
3 tablespoons heavy cream

SERVES 6.

Put the carrots in a pan with the butter, salt, sugar, and water to cover. Bring to a boil and then cook, uncovered, over moderate heat 20 minutes or until the liquid is syrupy and the carrots are tender.

The carrots can be cooked ahead and kept, covered, in the refrigerator up to 3 days.

To finish: Make the béchamel sauce (13). Add the béchamel and heavy cream to the carrots and heat, stirring occasionally, until warm. Taste for seasoning before serving.

Stuffed Tomatoes
(TOMATES FARCIES)

"The beauty of this old-fashioned dish is its flexibility," says Léon. You can use almost any ingredient for the stuffing: Choose beef, pork, chicken, ham, sausage, liver, or fish for the meat; cooked rice instead of the bread crumbs, or even well-seasoned rice or macaroni in place of both the meat and the bread crumbs.

    4 large tomatoes, to stuff
    salt and pepper
    2 tablespoons olive oil
    1 medium onion, chopped
    1 garlic clove, chopped
    1 large tomato, peeled, seeded, and coarsely chopped
    ½ cup (50 g) dry bread crumbs, soaked in chicken stock (5),
        milk, or water and squeezed dry
    3 ounces (90 g) cooked ground or finely chopped meat (beef,
        pork, chicken, etc.)
    1 egg yolk
    ¼ cup (30 g) grated Parmesan cheese
    1 tablespoon chopped parsley
    ¼ teaspoon grated nutmeg
    1 tablespoon toasted bread crumbs
    olive oil (for sprinkling)

SERVES 4.

198

Slice off the tops of the tomatoes. Scoop out all the seeds and drain the juices from the cavities. Season the cavities with salt and pepper.

In a sauté pan heat the oil and cook the onion until soft but not brown. Add the garlic and the chopped tomato pulp and cook 2–3 minutes. Add the ½ cup (50 g) bread crumbs and the meat. Cook, stirring, 2–3 minutes until hot. Remove the pan from the heat and add the egg yolk, stirring well. It will cook and thicken the mixture slightly. Stir in the Parmesan, parsley, nutmeg, and salt and pepper to taste. The tomatoes can be prepared 24 hours ahead and kept, covered, in the refrigerator.

Preheat the oven to 375°F (190°C). Fill the tomatoes with the stuffing. Sprinkle each with dry bread crumbs and a few drops of olive oil. Bake, uncovered, for 15 minutes and serve.

Eggplant Italienne
(AUBERGINES À L'ITALIENNE)

Cooks of all nations enjoy this Italian-inspired preparation for egg-plant.

> 3 medium eggplants
> salt
> tomato sauce (18) made with 2 tablespoons (30 g) butter, 1 onion, chopped, 1½ tablespoons (12 g) flour, 1 cup (250 ml) white veal (4) or chicken (5) stock OR stock and tomato juice, 1½ pounds (750 g) tomatoes, 1 garlic clove, bouquet garni (1), ¼ teaspoon sugar, and salt and pepper
> ½ cup (65 g) flour
> oil (for frying)
> 1 cup (100 g) grated Gruyère cheese
> 2 tablespoons (30 g) butter

SERVES 4.

Peel the eggplants, slice them into ½-inch (1.25 cm) rounds, and sprinkle lightly with salt. Put them in a colander to drain for ½ hour. Make the tomato sauce (18). Rinse the eggplant slices and then dry on paper towels. Dredge them in flour, sauté in hot oil until golden brown, and drain.

In a buttered casserole layer the eggplant slices alternately with the tomato sauce, grated cheese, and pieces of butter. The eggplant can be prepared a day ahead and kept, covered, in the refrigerator.

To finish: Bake in a preheated 400°F (200°F) oven for 20 minutes or until hot and brown, or brown under the broiler.

Strawberry Charlotte Malakoff
(CHARLOTTE MALAKOFF AUX FRAISES)

A malakoff mixture is always based on ground almonds. It can be flavored with kirsch, with coffee, with candied fruits and Cointreau, or, as here, with strawberries.

12–14 ladyfingers (31) made with 6 tablespoons (55 g) flour, a pinch of salt, 2 eggs, ¼ cup (50 g) sugar, ¼ teaspoon vanilla extract, and powdered sugar
1 cup (180 g) whole blanched almonds
2 cups (200 g) fresh strawberries
¼ cup (60 ml) kirsch
¼ pound (125 g) butter
⅔ cup (135 g) sugar
½ cup (125 ml) heavy cream, lightly whipped
raspberry sauce (see Peaches Cardinal, p. 57) made with 1 quart (500 g) raspberries, 1 tablespoon kirsch, and 4 tablespoons (35 g) powdered sugar
Chantilly cream (36) made with ½ cup (125 ml) heavy cream, 2 teaspoons sugar, and ½ teaspoon vanilla extract

5-cup (1.25 L) charlotte mold or soufflé dish
pastry bag with medium star tip

Serves 8.

Make the ladyfingers (31). Grind the almonds a few at a time in a blender or rotary cheese grater. Reserve 8 strawberries all of the same size and cut the rest into pieces. Butter the mold or dish, line the bottom with a circle of waxed paper, and butter. Line the sides with ladyfingers, trimming them to fit tightly. Sprinkle the remaining ladyfingers with 2 tablespoons of the kirsch.

Cream the butter, gradually beat in the sugar, and continue beating until very soft and light. Stir in the ground almonds, the remaining 2 tablespoons of the kirsch, and the cut strawberries. (Note: Do not beat, or the oil will be drawn out of the almonds.) Fold in the lightly whipped cream and spoon half the mixture into the mold. Cover with kirsch-soaked ladyfingers, add the remaining almond-strawberry mixture, and smooth the top. Cover and chill the charlotte at least 4 hours or until firmly set. It can be made 3–4 days ahead and kept, covered, in the refrigerator. Make the raspberry sauce (see p. 57) and chill.

To finish: Not more than 2 hours before serving, trim the ends of the ladyfingers around the mold level with the filling. Unmold the charlotte onto a platter. Make the Chantilly cream and with the pastry bag pipe rosettes around the bottom and on the top of the charlotte. Decorate with the whole strawberries and serve with the raspberry sauce.

Caramel-glazed Puffs
(SALAMBÔS)

Salambôs are a charming variation on the well-known éclair. The choux pastry is shaped into small ovals instead of the traditional éclair shape, and caramel replaces the usual topping of chocolate or coffee fondant.

> choux pastry (**26**) made with ¾ cup (95 g) flour, ¾ cup (185 ml) water, ½ teaspoon salt, 5 tablespoons (80 g) butter, and 3–4 eggs
> 1 egg beaten with ½ teaspoon salt (for glaze)
> pastry cream (**34**) made with 6 egg yolks, ½ cup (100 g) sugar, ⅓ cup (45 g) flour, 2 cups (500 ml) milk, and 1–2 tablespoons kirsch or rum
> 2 tablespoons blanched pistachios, finely chopped

> *For the caramel:*
> ¾ cup (150 g) sugar
> ¼ cup (60 ml) water

> *pastry bag with ½-inch (1.25 cm) and ¼-inch (6 mm) plain tips*

MAKES about 20 salambôs.

Preheat the oven to 400°F (200°C). Make the choux pastry (**26**). Using the larger tip, pipe 1½-inch (4 cm) ovals of the dough well apart on a baking sheet, or shape the ovals with a tablespoon. Brush with the egg glaze and mark diagonal lines on the tops with a fork dipped in water. If using an unventilated electric oven, prop the door open slightly with a wooden spoon. Bake 20–25 minutes or until the puffs are firm and brown. Transfer to a rack to cool. The puffs can be kept overnight in an airtight container, but they are at their best eaten within a few hours.

Make the pastry cream (**34**), flavoring it with kirsch or rum, and rub a piece of butter on the top to prevent a skin from forming.

For the caramel: Heat the sugar with the water until dissolved, then boil without stirring until it is a light golden caramel color. Plunge the bottom of the pan into a bowl of warm water to stop cooking. Working quickly, dip the top of each puff into the caramel and immediately sprinkle with a pinch of chopped pistachios. If the caramel sets before all are coated, warm it gently but do not cook it further. The pastry cream can be made and the puffs can be coated 4–5 hours before serving. Keep the puffs in a dry place.

Not more than 2 hours before serving, put the pastry cream into the pastry bag fitted with the smaller tip. Make a slit in the side of each puff and fill with pastry cream. If keeping longer than 2 hours, refrigerate the puffs. They are best eaten the same day while still crisp.

Crêpes Creole
(CRÊPES CRÉOLE)

Bananas and rum give these crêpes their Creole accent.

crêpes (32) made with 1 cup (130 g) flour, ¼ teaspoon salt, 1 cup (250 ml) milk, 3 eggs, 2 tablespoons melted butter or oil, 1 tablespoon rum, and 5 tablespoons (80 g) clarified butter or oil (for frying)
2–3 tablespoons (20–25 g) sugar
¼ cup (60 ml) rum

For the filling:
2 tablespoons (30 g) butter
4 bananas, diced
2 tablespoons (25 g) sugar
6 tablespoons (115 g) apricot jam
1 tablespoon rum

MAKES about 18 crêpes, 6 servings.

Make the crêpes (32), adding the rum with the melted butter or oil.

For the filling: Not more than 3–4 hours before serving, melt the butter in a frying pan, add the bananas, and sprinkle with the 2 tablespoons (25 g) sugar. Cook over medium heat 1–2 minutes until lightly caramelized. Take from the heat and stir in the apricot jam and the 1 tablespoon rum. Put a spoonful of the mixture on each crêpe, roll it up like a cigar, and arrange the rolls diagonally in a shallow buttered baking dish.

To finish: Sprinkle the crêpes with the 2–3 tablespoons (20–25 g) sugar and broil 1–2 minutes or until they are very hot and beginning to caramelize on top. Heat the ¼ cup (60 ml) rum in a small pan, pour it over the crêpes, and flame. Serve at once.

Basic Recipes

THE BASIC RECIPES in this chapter are building blocks that form the foundations of other dishes. Almost always, basic recipes are used as they stand, but occasionally the proportions of ingredients may be changed for the special purposes of an individual recipe. For example, less sugar may be used to reduce the sweetness of a gâteau, extra egg yolks may enrich a custard, or a flavoring may be adjusted. Be sure to follow the quantities specified in the individual recipes, but the method of preparation of the basic recipe is always the same, as given in this chapter.

NOTE: The basic-recipe titles are coded with bold numerals in parentheses that you will also see—smaller, but again in bold type—in the lists of ingredients and in the text of individual recipes throughout the book, such as: chicken stock (**5**).

(1) Bouquet Garni

A bouquet garni is familiar—simply herbs tied together so they can be lifted out of the pot easily once their flavor has been transferred to the dish. Variations include the addition of celery or leeks, and the bouquet can be tied in cheesecloth rather than with string. Here is the basic bouquet garni:

1 sprig thyme, fresh or dried
1 bay leaf
10–12 parsley stems

Hold the thyme and bay leaf together and surround them with the parsley stems. Wind a piece of fine string around the parsley and tie it securely.

Stocks

(2) Brown Veal Stock
(FOND BRUN DE VEAU)

Note that salt is not normally added to any kind of stock, since the liquid is often very much reduced at the end of cooking and could become too salty.

Brown veal stock is used for brown sauces, ragoûts, and braised dishes.

4–5 pounds (2 kg) veal bones, cracked or cut into pieces
2 onions, quartered
2 carrots, quartered
2 stalks celery, cut into 2-inch (5 cm) pieces
1 large bouquet garni (**1**)

10 peppercorns
1 unpeeled garlic clove
3–4 quarts (3–4 L) water
1 tablespoon tomato paste
½ onion—optional

MAKES 2–3 quarts (2–3 L) stock.

Preheat the oven to 450°F (230°C.) Put the bones in a roasting pan and roast them, stirring occasionally, for 30–40 minutes or until they are browned. Add the vegetables and brown them also. With a metal spoon, transfer the bones and vegetables to a stockpot, leaving the fat behind. Add the bouquet garni, peppercorns, garlic, enough water to cover generously, and the tomato paste. Bring slowly to a boil, skimming often. (NOTE: To add color to the stock, singe half a cut onion over an electric or gas burner and add to the stock.) Simmer the stock 4–5 hours, skimming occasionally; it should reduce very slowly.

Strain the stock, taste, and, if the flavor is not concentrated, boil it until well reduced. Chill quickly by placing the container of stock in a basin of cold running water or ice and skim off any fat before using. Stock can be kept 4 days in the refrigerator. To keep it longer, boil it again 5–10 minutes, then chill again, and keep for another 3–4 days. It can also be frozen.

(3) Brown Beef Stock
(FOND BRUN DE BOEUF)

Beef stock is used for full-flavored sauces and for game dishes. It has a more mellow flavor than brown veal stock but less body, because beef bones contain less gelatin than veal.

Make exactly as brown veal stock (2), except use 2 pounds (1 kg) beef bones and 2 pounds (1 kg) veal bones.

(4) White Veal Stock
(FOND BLANC DE VEAU)

White veal stock is used for lighter sauces and is served with veal and poultry.

4–5 pounds (2 kg) veal bones, cracked or cut into pieces
2 onions, quartered
2 carrots, quartered
2 stalks celery, cut into 2-inch (5 cm) pieces
1 large bouquet garni (1)
10 peppercorns
1 unpeeled garlic clove
3–4 quarts (3–4 L) water

MAKES 2–3 quarts (2–3 L) stock.

Blanch the bones by bringing them to a boil in water to cover and then simmering 5 minutes. Drain and rinse in cold water. Put the bones and vegetables in a stockpot. Add the bouquet garni, peppercorns, garlic, and enough water to cover generously. Bring slowly to a boil, skimming often. Simmer 4–5 hours, skimming occasionally; it should reduce very slowly.

Strain the stock, taste, and, if the flavor isn't concentrated, boil until well reduced. Chill quickly by placing the container of stock in a basin of cold running water or ice and skim off any fat before using. Store in the refrigerator up to 4 days. To keep 3–4 days longer, boil the stock again for 5–10 minutes and then chill again. The stock can be frozen.

(5) Chicken Stock
(FOND DE VOLAILLE)

Chicken stock is used for poultry dishes and sauces.

Follow the recipe for white veal stock (4), using 3 pounds (1.5 kg) chicken backs and necks, or a whole chicken and 2 pounds (1 kg) veal bones. Simmer the stock 3–4 hours. The whole chicken can be removed after 1½ hours, or when tender, to use in another recipe. If it is left in for the full cooking time, it will give more flavor to the stock but the chicken meat will not be worth eating.

(6) Fish Stock
(FUMET DE POISSON)

Fish stock is used for fish sauces and soups. Be sure to simmer rather than boil the stock, or it will become cloudy and bitter.

1 medium onion, sliced
1 tablespoon (15 g) butter
1½ pounds (750 g) fish bones, broken into pieces
1 quart (1 L) water
10 peppercorns
1 bouquet garni (1)
1 cup (250 ml) dry white wine OR juice of ½ lemon—optional

MAKES about 1 quart (1 L) stock.

In a kettle cook the onion slowly in the butter until soft but not brown. Add the fish bones, water, peppercorns, bouquet garni, and wine or lemon juice. Bring slowly to a boil, skimming occasionally, and simmer, uncovered, 20 minutes. Strain and cool. Fish stock can be kept for 1 day in the refrigerator, or it can be frozen.

(7) Court Bouillon
(COURT BOUILLON)

Court bouillon is used for poaching fish, shellfish, and some variety meats.

1 quart (1 L) water
1 carrot, sliced
1 small onion, sliced
1 bouquet garni (1)
6 peppercorns
1 teaspoon salt
1 cup (250 ml) dry white wine OR ⅓ cup (30 ml) vinegar OR ¼
    cup (60 ml) lemon juice

MAKES 1 quart (1 L) court bouillon.

Combine all the ingredient in a pan (not aluminum), cover, and bring to a boil. Simmer, uncovered, for 20–30 minutes and strain.

(8) Meat, Chicken, or Fish Aspic
(GELÉE DE VIANDE, DE VOLAILLE, OU DE POISSON)

The color of aspic should range from very pale for fish, to a light gold for coating veal and chicken, to rich golden brown for the beef aspic used for red meats and game.

1½ quarts (1.5 L) well-flavored beef (3), veal (4), chicken (5),
    OR fish (6) stock
½–1 ounce (15–30 g) gelatin—optional
2 carrots, chopped
green tops of 2 leeks, chopped
2 stalks celery, chopped
2 tomatoes, quartered

212

7 ounces (200 g) finely chopped lean raw beef (for meat or
    chicken aspic) OR finely chopped raw fish (for fish aspic)
3 egg whites, beaten until frothy
¼ cup (60 ml) Madeira or sherry
salt and pepper

MAKES about 1 quart (1 L) aspic.

The stock must be firmly set. If not, be ready to add to it ½–1
ounce (15–30 g) gelatin, depending on whether it is lightly set or
almost liquid. Sprinkle the gelatin over ½ cup (125 ml) of cold stock
in a small bowl and leave 5 minutes or until spongy. Add it to the
stock as directed later on in the recipe.

Skim all the fat from the stock, heat it in a large pan (not aluminum), and remove any remaining fat by pulling strips of paper
towel across the surface.

In a bowl mix the carrots, leeks, celery, tomatoes, chopped beef
or fish, and beaten egg whites. Pour on the warm stock, whisking, and
return the mixture to the pan. Set the pan over moderate heat and
bring slowly to a boil, whisking constantly—this should take about
10 minutes.

As soon as the mixture looks milky, stop whisking. (NOTE: Continued whisking would prevent the formation of the filter of egg
whites.) Let the filter rise slowly to the top of the pan, then turn
down the heat. With a ladle, make a small hole in the egg-white filter,
so the aspic bubbles through the filter only in that place; otherwise
the filter may break.

Let the aspic simmer gently 30–40 minutes to extract the flavor
from the vegetables and the meat or fish and to allow the liquid time
to clarify. Now, if needed, carefully add the gelatin through the hole
in the filter; simmer gently 2–3 minutes to be sure it is dissolved. Add
the Madeira or sherry. Taste the aspic for seasoning and adjust if
necessary.

Place a scalded dish towel or jelly bag in a strainer over a clean
bowl and ladle the aspic into it, beginning where the hole was made
in the filter. Do not press on the vegetables, meat, or fish left in the
towel. If the aspic running through is not sparkling clear, strain it
again through the towel and the filter of ingredients and egg white

deposited in the towel. Leave the aspic to cool. It can be kept 1–2 days in the refrigerator. Pour a layer of water over the aspic after it has set to prevent a skin from forming.

Sauces

(9) Basic Brown Sauce
(FOND DE VEAU LIÉ)

This is a streamlined version of the classic espagnole sauce. It can be used as a base for all brown sauces and has largely replaced espagnole in the modern kitchen.

> 3 cups (750 ml) well-flavored brown veal stock (**2**)
> 2 tablespoons (20 g) arrowroot or potato starch
> 4 tablespoons Madeira or water
> salt and pepper

MAKES 3 cups (750 ml) sauce.

Bring the stock to a boil. Mix the arrowroot or potato starch to a paste with the Madeira or cold water. Pour some or all of the mixture into the stock, whisking constantly, adding enough to thicken the sauce to the desired consistency. Bring it back to a boil, taste for seasoning, and adjust if necessary. Strain through a fine sieve. Rub the surface of the warm sauce with butter to prevent a skin from forming. The sauce can be kept, covered, 3–4 days in the refrigerator.

NOTE: For a richer version of basic brown sauce, brown 1 onion and 1 carrot, both diced, in 3 tablespoons (45 g) butter. Add 1 tomato, diced, 1 tablespoon tomato paste, and the stock. Simmer 30 minutes and then continue as above.

Basic Recipes

Brown Sauce Derivatives (DÉRIVÉS DES SAUCES BRUNES):

(10) Demi-glace Sauce

Full-flavored demi-glace sauce is served with meats and can be a base for other sauces.

To 2 cups (500 ml) basic brown sauce (9) add 4 tablespoons chopped mushrooms, 2 teaspoons tomato paste, ¼ cup (60 ml) brown veal stock (2) or beef stock (3), and ¼ cup (60 ml) Madeira. Simmer, skimming often, until reduced to about 2 cups (500 ml) and take from the heat. Taste for seasoning and adjust if necessary. Whisk in 2 tablespoons (30 g) butter in small pieces.

(11) Madeira Sauce
(SAUCE MADÈRE)

Madeira sauce is traditionally served with variety meats, beef fillet, veal, and ham.

Bring 2 cups (500 ml) demi-glace sauce (10) to a boil, take from the heat, and add 3 tablespoons Madeira (or to taste). Alternatively, simmer 3 tablespoons Madeira with 2 cups (500 ml) basic brown sauce (13) 8–10 minutes, take from the heat, and add 3 tablespoons more Madeira (or to taste). Taste for seasoning and adjust if necessary.

(12) *Pepper Sauce*
(SAUCE POIVRADE)

This peppery sauce is especially good with broiled beef.

Sauté 2 tablespoons each of diced onion, carrot, and celery in 3 tablespoons (45 g) butter or oil. Add 1 cup (250 ml) white-wine vinegar and a bouquet garni (1) and reduce to ¼ cup (60 ml.) Add 2 cups (500 ml) basic brown sauce (9) and simmer 10–15 minutes, skimming often. Strain the sauce, stir in 1 tablespoon (15 g) butter, and season well with pepper. (NOTE: A different sauce poivrade is often made with the marinade from game.)

(13) *Béchamel Sauce*
(SAUCE BÉCHAMEL)

The simplest of the basic sauces, béchamel can be made from supplies always on hand. It is made thin, medium, and thick for different purposes, and, of course, it is simply the old-fashioned "cream sauce" we have always known, seasoned, by the French, with special care.

1 cup (250 ml) milk
1 slice of onion—optional
1 small bay leaf—optional
6 peppercorns—optional
salt and white pepper
pinch of grated nutmeg

For the roux:
Thin: 1 tablespoon (15 g) butter
      1 tablespoon (8 g) flour
Medium: 1½ tablespoons (20 g) butter
        1½ tablespoons (12 g) flour

Thick: 2 tablespoons (30 g) butter
      2 tablespoons (15 g) flour

MAKES 1 cup (250 ml) sauce.

Scald the milk in a saucepan. Add the onion, bay leaf, and peppercorns, cover, and leave in a warm place 5–10 minutes. Meanwhile make the roux: In a heavy-bottomed saucepan melt the butter, whisk in the flour, and cook 1–2 minutes until the roux is foaming but not browned; let it cool. Strain in the hot milk, whisking, then bring the sauce to a boil, whisking constantly, and add salt, pepper, and nutmeg to taste. Simmer 3–5 minutes. If the sauce is not used at once, rub the surface with butter to prevent a skin from forming. Béchamel can be kept, covered, 2–3 days in the refrigerator.

Béchamel Sauce Derivatives (DÉRIVÉS DE SAUCE BÉCHAMEL):

(14) Mornay Sauce
(SAUCE MORNAY)

This versatile cheese-flavored sauce can be served with eggs, fish, poultry, white meats, and vegetables.

Make 1 cup (250 ml) thin béchamel sauce (13). Take from the heat and beat in 1 egg yolk (optional) and ¼ cup (25–30 g) grated cheese. (NOTE: Well-aged Gruyère or Parmesan, or a mixture of both, are the best cheeses to use.) Do not reheat the sauce or the cheese will cook into strings. Off the heat, stir in 1 tablespoon (15 g) butter. The sauce can be flavored with 1 teaspoon Dijon mustard. Taste for seasoning and adjust if necessary.

(15) Soubise Sauce
(SAUCE SOUBISE)

Soubise sauce is good for eggs, veal, and lamb.

Make 1 cup (250 ml) thick béchamel sauce (13). Chop 2 medium onions, blanch them 1 minute in boiling salted water, and drain. Melt 2 tablespoons (30 g) butter in a heavy-bottomed pan and add the onions and salt and pepper. Top the onions with a piece of waxed paper and cover the pan with the lid. Cook very gently 10–15 minutes until they are very soft but not brown. Stir the onions into the sauce and work the mixture through a fine strainer. Reheat the sauce, stir in 2 tablespoons heavy cream, taste for seasoning, and adjust if necessary.

(16) Velouté Sauce
(LE VELOUTÉ)

Velouté sauce can be flavored with veal, chicken, or fish stock, and it is often made with the cooking liquid from the food it accompanies.

> 1 cup (250 ml) well-flavored white veal (4), chicken (5), or fish (6) stock
> 1½ tablespoons (20 g) butter
> 1½ tablespoons (12 g) flour
> salt and pepper

Makes 1 cup (250 ml) sauce.

Bring the stock to a boil. In a heavy-bottomed saucepan melt the butter, whisk in the flour, and cook 1–2 minutes until the roux is foaming but not browned. Let cool and then gradually whisk in the hot stock. Bring the sauce to a boil, whisking constantly, and add only a little salt and pepper—the flavor of the sauce will be concentrated during later cooking. Simmer, skimming occasionally for 10–20 minutes, or longer if necessary, until it has the required consistency. Taste again for seasoning and adjust if necessary. If the sauce is not used at once, rub the surface with butter to prevent a skin from forming. Velouté can be kept, covered, in the refrigerator for 2–3 days.

Velouté Sauce Derivative (DÉRIVÉ DE SAUCE VELOUTÉ):

(17) Allemande Sauce
(SAUCE ALLEMANDE)

Serve this mushroom-flavored sauce with veal, poultry, and vegetables.

While simmering 1 cup (250 ml) veal velouté sauce (**16**), add ¼ cup (60 ml) chopped mushroom stems. Strain the sauce and whisk in 1 egg yolk. Bring the sauce back just to a boil, season it to taste, and add a squeeze of lemon juice and a pinch of grated nutmeg. Take from the heat and add 2 tablespoons (30 g) butter.

(18) Tomato Sauce
(SAUCE TOMATE)

Unless fresh tomatoes are ripe and glowing red, tomato sauce made with canned Italian-style tomatoes has more flavor.

2 tablespoons (30 g) butter
1 onion, chopped

2 tablespoons (15 g) flour
1½ cups (375 ml) white veal (4) or chicken (5) stock OR stock
    mixed with juice from canned tomatoes
2 pounds (1 kg) fresh tomatoes, quartered, OR 3 cups (1½ pounds
    or 750 g) canned tomatoes, drained and chopped
1 garlic clove, crushed
1 bouquet garni (1)
½ teaspoon sugar
salt and pepper
2 tablespoons tomato paste—optional

MAKES about 2½ cups (625 ml) sauce.

In a saucepan melt the butter and cook the onion slowly until soft nut brown. Stir in the flour and cook 1–2 minutes until foaming. Off the heat, pour in the stock, then bring to a boil, stirring. Add the tomatoes, garlic, bouquet garni, sugar, and salt and pepper to taste. Simmer uncovered, stirring occasionally, for 30–40 minutes for canned tomatoes and 45–60 minutes for fresh tomatoes, or until the tomatoes are very soft and the sauce is slightly thick.

Work the sauce through a strainer, pressing well to extract all the tomato purée, and return it to the pan. Reheat it and, if too thin, reduce. If the sauce has been made from fresh tomatoes and a darker color is desired, add the tomato paste. Taste the sauce for seasoning and adjust if necessary. Rub the surface of the warm sauce with butter to prevent a skin from forming. It can be kept, covered, 2–3 days in the refrigerator, or it can be frozen.

(19) Stewed Tomato Pulp
(COULIS DE TOMATES)

Stewed tomato pulp is added to sauces and stuffings.

2 tablespoons oil
1 shallot OR ½ small onion, finely chopped

2 pounds (1 kg) fresh tomatoes, peeled, seeded, and chopped
1 small bouquet garni (**1**)
salt and pepper

Makes about 2 cups (500 ml) pulp.

Heat the oil, add the chopped shallot or onion, and cook slowly, stirring often, for 3–5 minutes or until soft but not brown. Add the tomatoes, bouquet garni, salt and pepper and cook over medium heat, stirring frequently, for 20–30 minutes or until nearly all the moisture has evaporated. Taste for seasoning and adjust if necessary. Tomato pulp can be kept, covered, for 2–3 days in the refrigerator, or it can be frozen.

(20) Hollandaise Sauce
(SAUCE HOLLANDAISE)

Hollandaise sauce is served with poached fish, vegetables, and eggs.

6 ounces (180 g) butter
3 tablespoons water
3 egg yolks
salt and white pepper
juice of ½ lemon, or to taste

Makes about 1 cup (250 ml) sauce.

Melt the butter, skim any froth from the surface, and let cool to tepid. In a small heavy-bottomed saucepan whisk the water and egg yolks with a little salt and pepper for 30 seconds or until light. Set the pan over low heat or in a water bath and whisk constantly until the mixture is creamy and thick enough so the whisk leaves a trail on the bottom of the pan. The bottom of the pan should never be more than hand-hot.

Take from the heat and whisk in the tepid butter a few drops at a time. (Note: Do not add the butter too quickly or the sauce may separate.) When the sauce has started to thicken, the butter can be added a little faster. Do not add the milky sediment at the bottom of the butter. When all the butter is added, stir in the lemon juice and add salt, pepper, and lemon juice to taste. Hollandaise is served warm, not hot, and it should be kept warm over hot water to avoid separation.

If hollandaise does separate, this is almost always because it is too hot; take it at once from the heat and whisk in an ice cube. If this is not successful, the sauce can be started again by whisking an egg yolk and a tablespoon of water over low heat until creamy and then gradually whisking in the separated mixture drop by drop. However, if the sauce is badly curdled, the egg yolks have cooked into granules and the mixture must be discarded. Very occasionally hollandaise separates due to undercooking—never having thickened properly. If so, try whisking in a tablespoon of boiling water. If hollandaise is too thick add 1 tablespoon tepid water to make it lighter.

(21) Béarnaise Sauce
(SAUCE BÉARNAISE)

Béarnaise is made in exactly the same way as hollandaise sauce (20), and the same notes apply about preventing it from separating and keeping it warm. Béarnaise is served with steak, lamb, and rich fish such as salmon.

    6 ounces (180 g) butter
    3 tablespoons vinegar
    3 tablespoons dry white wine
    10 peppercorns, crushed
    2 shallots, finely chopped
    1 tablespoon chopped fresh tarragon stems or tarragon leaves
        preserved in vinegar
    3 egg yolks

salt and white or cayenne pepper
1 tablespoon chopped chervil or parsley
1–2 tablespoons finely chopped fresh tarragon or tarragon leaves
  preserved in vinegar (to finish)

MAKES about 1 cup (250 ml) sauce.

Melt the butter, skim any froth from the surface, and let cool to tepid. In a small, heavy-bottomed saucepan boil the vinegar and wine with the peppercorns, chopped shallots, and the 1 tablespoon tarragon stems or leaves until reduced to 2 tablespoons. Let cool. Add the egg yolks and a little salt and pepper and whisk for 30 seconds or until light. Set the pan over low heat or in a water bath and whisk constantly until the mixture is creamy and quite thick, thicker than for hollandaise. The bottom of the pan should never be more than hand-hot. Take from the heat and whisk in the tepid butter, a few drops at a time. When the sauce has thickened, the butter can be added more quickly. Do not add the milky sediment at the bottom of the pan.

When all the butter is added, strain, pressing hard to extract all the sauce. Add the chervil or parsley and the chopped tarragon and taste for seasoning. Béarnaise should be quite piquant with pepper.

(22) *White Butter Sauce*
(SAUCE BEURRE BLANC)

White butter sauce originated in the Loire Valley and traditionally is made with the local Muscadet wine and served with pike from the local rivers. It resembles hollandaise and béarnaise sauces, but it is more delicate, as it is made very simply of butter whisked into a reduction of wine, vinegar, and shallots.

  3 tablespoons white-wine vinegar
  3 tablespoons dry white wine
  2 shallots, finely chopped

¼ pound (250 g) cold butter
salt and white pepper

MAKES 1 cup (250 ml) sauce.

In a small saucepan (not aluminum) boil the wine vinegar, wine, and shallots until reduced to 1 tablespoon. Set the pan over low heat and whisk in the butter gradually in small pieces to make a smooth, creamy sauce. Work sometimes over low heat and sometimes off the heat, so that the butter softens and thickens the sauce without melting. Season to taste with salt and white pepper and serve as soon as possible—if kept warm, the sauce may melt. If it must be kept warm for a few minutes, keep it on a rack above warm, but not boiling, water.

(23) *Mayonnaise*
(MAYONNAISE)

All ingredients must be at room temperature or the mayonnaise will not emulsify. If the oil is cold, heat it just to tepid and, on a cold day, warm the bowl and whisk in hot water before beginning.

2 egg yolks
salt and white pepper
1–2 tablespoons white-wine vinegar OR lemon juice
¼ teaspoon dry mustard or Dijon mustard, or to taste—optional
1½ cups (375 ml) oil

MAKES about 1½ cups (375 ml) mayonnaise.

Using a whisk or an electric beater, beat the egg yolks in a small bowl with a little salt and pepper, 1 tablespoon of the vinegar or lemon juice, and the mustard until thick. Add the oil drop by drop whisking constantly. (NOTE: If oil is added too quickly, the mayonnaise will separate.) When 2 tablespoons of the oil have been added, the mixture should be very thick. The remaining oil can be added a little more quickly, either 1 tablespoon at a time, thoroughly beating between each addition until it is absorbed, or in a thin, steady stream if an electric mixer is being used.

When all the oil has been added, stir in the remaining vinegar or lemon juice to taste, more mustard, and salt and white pepper as needed. The amount of seasoning depends very much on the oil and vinegar used and what dish the mayonnaise is to accompany. If necessary, thin the mayonnaise with a little warm water.

Mayonnaise is best eaten very soon and never refrigerated. But if it is stored in the refrigerator, it should be brought to room temperature before stirring, otherwise it may separate. It can be kept 2–3 days.

If mayonnaise does separate during making, or on standing, beat in a tablespoon of boiling water. If it does not re-emulsify, start again by beating a fresh egg yolk with salt and pepper and then whisking in the curdled mixture drop by drop. Alternatively, if the mayonnaise is flavored with mustard, the separated mixture can be gradually beaten into another bowl containing a teaspoonful of Dijon mustard.

Pastry & Cakes

(24) Pie Pastry
(PÂTE BRISÉE)

This basic pie pastry is suitable for either sweet or savory dishes.

To make *one* 7–8-inch (18–20 cm) pie shell
OR *four* 4-inch (10 cm) tartlet shells:

1 cup (130 g) flour
4 tablespoons (60 g) unsalted butter
1 egg yolk
¼ teaspoon salt
3–4 tablespoons cold water

To make *one* 9–10-inch (23–25 cm) pie shell
OR *six* 4-inch (10 cm) tartlet shells:

1½ cups (195 g) flour
6 tablespoons (95 g) unsalted butter
1 egg yolk
½ teaspoon salt
4–5 tablespoons cold water

To make *one* 11–12-inch (28–30 cm) pie shell
OR *eight* 4-inch (10 cm) tartlet shells:

2 cups (260 g) flour
¼ pound (125 g) unsalted butter
2 egg yolks
¾ teaspoon salt
5–6 tablespoons cold water

Sift the flour onto a working surface and make a large well in the center. Pound the butter with a rolling pin to soften it slightly. Put the butter, egg yolk(s), salt, and smaller amount of water in the well and stir together with the fingertips of one hand until partly mixed. Gradually work in the flour, pulling the dough into large crumbs with the fingertips of both hands. If the crumbs are dry, sprinkle over another tablespoon water. Press the dough together—it should be soft but not sticky. Now work the dough on a lightly floured surface, pushing it away with the heel of the hand and gathering it up with a dough scraper until it is smooth and pliable. Press the dough into a ball, wrap, and chill 30 minutes. It can be stored, tightly wrapped, in the refrigerator for up to 3 days.

(25) Sweet Pie Pastry
(PÂTE SUCRÉE)

A cookie-like dough, sweet and crisp, that makes an ideal pastry for fruit tarts.

To make *one* 7–8-inch (18–20 cm) pie shell
OR *four* 4-inch (10 cm) tartlet shells:

¾ cup (95 g) flour
¼ teaspoon salt
4 tablespoons (60 g) sugar
2 egg yolks
½ teaspoon vanilla extract
4 tablespoons (60 g) unsalted butter

To make *one* 9–10-inch (23–25 cm) pie shell
OR *six* 4-inch (10 cm) tartlet shells:

1 cup (130 g) flour
⅓ teaspoon salt
⅓ cup (65 g) sugar
3 egg yolks
¾ teaspoon vanilla extract
5 tablespoons (80 g) unsalted butter

To make *one* 11–12-inch (28–30 cm) pie shell
OR *eight* 4-inch (10 cm) tartlet shells:

1½ cups (195 g) flour
½ teaspoon salt
½ cup (100 g) sugar
4 egg yolks
1 teaspoon vanilla extract
¼ pound (125 g) unsalted butter

Sift the flour onto a working surface and make a large well in the center. Put the salt, sugar, egg yolks, and vanilla extract in the well and mix them with your fingers until the sugar dissolves. Pound the butter with a rolling pin to soften it slightly, add it to the well, and quickly work it with the other ingredients until partly mixed. Gradually work in the flour, pulling the dough into large crumbs with the fingertips of both hands. Press the dough together—it should be soft but not sticky. Now work the dough on a lightly floured surface, pushing it away with the heel of the hand and gathering it up with a dough scraper until it is smooth and pliable. Press the dough into a ball, wrap, and chill 30 minutes. The dough can be stored, tightly wrapped, in the refrigerator for up to 3 days.

(26) Choux Pastry
(PÂTE À CHOUX)

When making the smallest quantity (with ½ cup or 65 g flour) of choux pastry, ingredients must be measured extremely accurately.

To make *fifteen* 3-inch (7.5 cm) baked puffs:

½ cup (65 g) flour
½ cup (125 ml) water
¼ teaspoon salt
4 tablespoons (60 g) unsalted butter
2 large eggs

To make *twenty* 3-inch (7.5 cm) baked puffs:

¾ cup (95 g) flour
¾ cup (185 ml) water
½ teaspoon salt
5 tablespoons (80 g) unsalted butter
3–4 large eggs

To make *twenty-five* 3-inch (7.5 cm) baked puffs:

1 cup (130 g) flour
1 cup (250 ml) water
¾ teaspoon salt
¼ pound (125 g) unsalted butter
4–5 large eggs

Sift the flour onto a piece of waxed paper. In a saucepan heat the water, salt, and butter until the butter is melted, then bring to a boil, and take from the heat. (NOTE: Prolonged boiling evaporates the water and changes the proportions of the dough.) As soon as the pan is taken from the heat, add all the flour at once and beat vigorously with a wooden spatula for a few seconds until the mixture is smooth and pulls away from the pan to form a ball. Beat ½–1 minute longer over low heat to dry the mixture.

Set aside 1 egg and beat it in a bowl. With a wooden spatula beat the remaining eggs into the dough one by one, beating thoroughly after each addition. Now beat enough of the reserved egg into the dough to make a mixture that is very shiny and just falls from the spoon. (NOTE: If too much egg is added, the dough cannot be shaped.)

Though the dough puffs better if it is used immediately, choux pastry can be stored up to 8 hours. Rub the surface with butter while the dough is still warm to prevent a skin from forming. When cool, cover tightly and store in the refrigerator.

(27) Puff Pastry
(PÂTE FEUILLETÉE)

For puff pastry it is important to work on a cold surface. If your working surface is warm, chill it by placing ice trays on top before making the détrempe and before every 2 turns. Dry the working surface well after removing the ice.

To make *one* 8-inch (20 cm) vol-au-vent
OR *nine–ten* 3-inch (7.5 cm) bouchées:

6 ounces–½ pound (180–250 g) unsalted butter
1⅓ cups (175 g) all-purpose flour
⅔ cup (80 g) cake flour
1 teaspoon salt
1 teaspoon lemon juice
½–¾ cup (125–185 ml) cold water

To make *one* 9-inch (23 cm) vol-au-vent
OR *thirteen–fifteen* 3-inch (7.5 cm) bouchées:

10 ounces–¾ pound (300–350 g) unsalted butter
2 cups (260 g) all-purpose flour
1 cup (120 g) cake flour
1½ teaspoons salt
1½ teaspoons lemon juice
¾–1 cup (185–250 ml) cold water

To make *one* 10-inch (25 cm) vol-au-vent
OR *eighteen–twenty* 3-inch (7.5 cm) bouchées:

¾–1 pound (350–500 g) unsalted butter
2⅔ cups (350 g) all-purpose flour
1⅓ cups (160 g) cake flour
2 teaspoons salt
2 teaspoons lemon juice
1¼–1½ cups (310–375 ml) cold water

Melt or soften ¹⁄₁₀ of the butter. Keep the rest of the butter cold. Sift the flour onto a cold surface, make a well in the center, and add the salt, lemon juice, the smaller amount of water, and the melted or softened butter. Work together with the fingertips until well mixed; then gradually work in the flour, pulling the dough into large crumbs using the fingertips of both hands. If the crumbs are dry, add more water—the amount of water needed depends on the flour used. Cut the dough several times with a dough scraper to ensure that the ingredients are evenly blended, but do not knead it. Press the dough to form a ball. It should be quite soft. This dough is called the détrempe. Wrap and chill it 15 minutes.

Basic Recipes

The amount of butter used depends on the desired richness of the dough and on your own experience. The usual practice is to use half the weight of the détrempe in butter, but you may use up to the maximum indicated in the recipe. Lightly flour the butter, flatten it with a rolling pin, and fold it in half. Continue pounding and folding it until it is pliable but not sticky—the butter should be the same consistency as the détrempe. Shape it into a 6-inch (15 cm) square. Roll out the dough on a floured surface to a 12-inch (30 cm) circle that is thicker in the center than at the sides. Set the butter in the center and fold the dough over it like an envelope. Pound the seams lightly to seal them.

Place the "package" of dough, seams down, on a well-floured working surface and tap the dough 3–4 times with the rolling pin to flatten it slightly. Roll it out to a rectangle 7–8 inches (18–20 cm) wide and 18–20 inches (45–50 cm) long. Fold the rectangle of dough in three, one end inside, as in folding a business letter, and align the layers as accurately as possible. Seal the edges with the rolling pin and turn the dough a quarter turn (90°) to bring the fold to your left, so that the dough could open like a book. This is called a "turn." Roll out again and fold in three. This is the second turn. Keep a note of these turns by marking the dough lightly with the appropriate number of fingerprints. Wrap the dough and chill 30 minutes.

Repeat the folding process, with the closed seam to your left, giving the dough 6 turns altogether, with a 30 minute rest in the refrigerator between every 2 turns. Chill at least 30 minutes before using.

Puff pastry that has had either 4 or 6 turns can be kept, tightly wrapped, in the refrigerator for up to 1 week, or for up to 3 months in the freezer. When making the pastry ahead, it is preferable to store it at 4 turns and to do the last 2 turns 30 minutes before shaping.

(28) Brioche
(BRIOCHE)

A normal quantity of yeast is given here, but up to 2 packages (30 g) of yeast can be used if the dough must rise as quickly as possible.

4 cups (520 g) flour
2½ teaspoons salt
2 tablespoons (25 g) sugar
1 package dry yeast OR 1 cake (15 g) compressed yeast
2 tablespoons lukewarm water
6–7 eggs
½ pound (250 g) unsalted butter

MAKES 15 small brioches OR 2 large (6-inch or 15 cm) loaves.

Sift the flour onto a working surface and make a large well in the center. Place the salt and sugar in little piles on one side of the well and the crumbled yeast opposite them, as far from the salt and sugar as possible. Pour the lukewarm water over the yeast and, using your fingertips, dilute the yeast in the water without mixing in the salt or sugar. Mix about one eighth of the flour into the yeast, still keeping the mixture on one side of the flour well. Leave to rise about 5–10 minutes.

Break in 5 of the eggs. With your fingers briefly mix the eggs with the salt, sugar, and yeast mixture; still using your fingertips, flick some of the flour over the center mixture so the center is no longer visible. Quickly draw in the rest of the flour with both hands, being careful not to let the liquid escape from the well. Pull the dough into large crumbs using the fingertips of both hands. Beat the sixth egg and add it. If the dough is dry, beat the remaining egg and add as much of it as necessary—the dough should be soft and sticky.

Mix the dough by pinching off 2 small portions between the thumb and forefinger of each hand and putting the portions removed on opposite ends of the mass of dough. Repeat this pinching motion about 5–7 times. Now knead the dough by lifting it up and slapping it down on the work surface for 5–10 minutes or until it is very smooth and elastic.

232

Pound the butter with a rolling pin to soften it thoroughly. Place the block of softened butter on the dough and mix it in with the same pinching motion used before. After 5–7 times, knead the dough by slapping it on the board as lightly as possible, just until the butter is completely incorporated. Roll very lightly in flour and shape into a smooth ball.

Transfer the dough to a lightly oiled bowl, turn the dough over, cover the bowl with a damp cloth, and let the dough rise at room temperature for about 2 hours or until nearly doubled in bulk. Remove to a floured surface and fold in three, patting it to knock out the air. Return to the bowl, cover with a damp cloth, and leave to rise at room temperature (or overnight in the refrigerator) until the dough is doubled in bulk. Brioche dough is much easier to handle if thoroughly chilled.

(29) Génoise
(GÉNOISE)

Though génoise is traditionally whisked over heat by hand, you need not heat the egg-and-sugar batter when using a powerful electric mixer. For a lighter, somewhat drier cake, substitute cake flour for all-purpose flour.

To make *one* 8–9-inch (20–23 cm) layer:

½ cup (65 g) flour
pinch salt—optional
3 tablespoons (45 g) butter—optional
3 eggs
½ cup (100 g) sugar

For flavoring—optional:
½ teaspoon vanilla extract
OR 1 teaspoon orange flower water
OR grated zest from 1 lemon or orange

To make *one* 9–10-inch (23–25 cm) layer:

¾ cup (95 g) flour
pinch salt—optional
4 tablespoons (60 g) butter—optional
4 eggs
⅔ cup (135 g) sugar

For flavoring—optional:
¾ teaspoon vanilla extract
OR 1½ teaspoons orange flower water
OR grated zest from 1½ lemon or orange

Brush the cake pan with melted butter. For extra protection against sticking, line the bottom with a circle of waxed paper that fits exactly and butter it also. Leave for a few minutes and then sprinkle the pan with flour. Shake to distribute the flour and discard the excess. Preheat the oven to 350°F (175°C).

Sift the flour with the salt 2–3 times. Clarify the 3 OR 4 tablespoons of butter by melting and then skimming the foam from the surface.

Put the eggs in a large bowl, preferably copper, and whisk in the sugar gradually. Set the bowl over a pan of hot but not boiling water, or over very low heat, and whisk 8–10 minutes or until the mixture is light and thick enough to leave a ribbon trail when the whisk is lifted. Take the bowl from the heat, add the chosen flavoring, and continue whisking until the mixture is cool. (NOTE: If using a powerful electric mixer, the mixture can be whisked in the mixer bowl over low heat until just warm and then beaten in the mixer at high speed until cool and thick enough to form a ribbon.)

Sift the flour over the batter in three batches, folding in each batch with a wooden spatula or metal spoon as lightly as possible. Right after the last batch, add the butter but don't pour in the milky sediment at the bottom of the pan. Fold in the last batch of flour and the butter together. (NOTE: The batter quickly loses volume after the butter is added.)

Pour the batter into the prepared cake pan and bake in the pre-heated oven, allowing 25–30 minutes for the smaller cake or 35–40 minutes for the larger one, or until the cake shrinks slightly from the sides of the pan and the top springs back when lightly pressed with a fingertip. Run a knife around the sides of the cake to loosen it and turn out onto a rack to cool.

Génoise can be kept several days in an airtight container, or it can be frozen.

(30) Sponge Cake
(BISCUIT)

Because the eggs are separated and the whites are beaten for sponge cake, it is lighter and drier than génoise.

To make *one* 8–9-inch (20–23 cm) layer:

½ cup (65 g) flour
pinch salt—optional
3 eggs, separated
½ cup (100 g) sugar

    For flavoring—optional:
½ teaspoon vanilla extract
OR 1 teaspoon orange flower water
OR grated zest from 1 lemon or orange

To make *one* 9–10-inch (23–25 cm) layer:

¾ cup (95 g) flour

pinch salt—optional
4 eggs, separated
¾ cup (150 g) sugar

For flavoring—optional:
¾ teaspoon vanilla extract
OR 1½ teaspoons orange flower water
OR grated zest from 1½ lemon or orange

Thoroughly brush the cake pan with melted butter. For extra protection against sticking, line the bottom with a circle of waxed paper that fits exactly and butter it also. Leave for a few minutes and then sprinkle the pan with flour. Shake to distribute the flour and discard the excess. Preheat the oven to moderate, (350°F or 175°C).

Sift the flour with the salt. Beat the egg yolks with half the sugar and the flavoring until the mixture is thick and light and leaves a thick ribbon trail when the whisk is lifted. Beat the egg whites, if possible in a copper bowl, until they are stiff. Add the rest of the sugar to the whites and beat 20–30 seconds longer or until glossy. As lightly as possible, fold the flour and egg whites alternately into the egg-yolk mixture, in 2–3 batches each, using a wooden spatula or metal spoon.

Pour the batter into the prepared pan and bake in the preheated oven, allowing 25–30 minutes for the smaller cake or 35–40 minutes for the larger one, or until the cake shrinks slightly from the sides of the pan and the top springs back when lightly pressed with a fingertip. Run a knife around the sides of the cake to loosen it and turn out onto a rack to cool.

The cake is best served fresh, but it can be kept a day or two in an airtight container. It freezes well.

(31) *Ladyfingers*
(BISCUITS À LA CUILLER)

Fresh ladyfingers are delicious as an accompaniment to ice cream but are most frequently seen on the French table as an essential part of a charlotte (see Chocolate Charlotte, p. 98; Strawberry Charlotte Malakoff, p. 200).

¾ cup (95 g) flour
tiny pinch of salt
4 eggs, separated
½ cup (100 g) sugar
½ teaspoon vanilla extract—optional
powdered sugar (for dusting)

pastry bag with ¾-inch (2 cm) plain tip

MAKES about 30 ladyfingers.

Preheat the oven to 350°F (175°C). Cover a baking sheet with parchment paper, or butter and flour the baking sheet lightly.

Sift the flour and salt together twice. Beat the egg yolks with half the sugar and the vanilla until light and thick enough to leave a ribbon trail. Beat the egg whites until stiff, add the remaining sugar, and beat 20 seconds longer or until glossy. Pour the sifted flour over the yolks and sugar and fold together as lightly as possible. Gently fold in the egg whites in 2 batches. (NOTE: The mixture must be folded as quickly as possible, but with great care, as it must remain stiff enough to pipe.)

Gently spoon the mixture into the pastry bag fitted with the plain tip and pipe fingers about 3½ inches (9 cm) long and 1 inch (2.5 cm) apart on the prepared baking sheet. Immediately sprinkle the tops with powdered sugar and gently shake off the excess. Bake in the preheated oven, with the door held slightly ajar by a wooden spoon, for 15–18 minutes or until light beige and firm on the outside but still soft in the center. Transfer to a rack to cool. Ladyfingers can be kept 3–4 days in an airtight container, or they can be frozen.

(32) Crêpes

Crêpe batter can, and in fact should, be made ahead. It thickens slightly on standing as the starch in the flour expands. Finished crêpes keep well, too.

To make *eighteen* crêpes 6–7 inches (15–18 cm) in diameter:

1 cup (130 g) flour
½ teaspoon salt
1 cup (250 ml) milk
3 eggs
2 tablespoons (30 g) melted butter or oil
5 tablespoons (80 g) clarified butter or oil (for frying)

To make *twenty-eight* crêpes 6–7 inches (15–18 cm) in diameter:

1½ cups (195 g) flour
¾ teaspoon salt
1½ cups (375 ml) milk
4 large eggs
3 tablespoons (45 g) melted butter or oil
¼ pound (125 g) clarified butter or oil (for frying)

Sift the flour into a bowl, make a well in the center, and add the salt and half the milk. Gradually whisk in the flour to make a smooth batter. Whisk in the eggs. (NOTE: Do not beat the batter too much, or it will become elastic and the finished crêpes will be tough.) Stir in the melted butter or oil with half the remaining milk, cover, and let the batter stand 1–2 hours. The batter can be kept up to 24 hours in the refrigerator.

Just before using, stir in enough of the remaining milk to make a batter the consistency of heavy cream. Brush or rub the crêpe pan with butter or oil and heat until very hot (a drop of batter will sizzle at once). Add 2–3 tablespoons of the batter to the hot pan, turning it quickly so the bottom is evenly coated. Cook over fairly high heat until browned and then toss the crêpe or turn it with a spatula. Cook for about 10 seconds to brown the other side and turn out onto a plate. Continue cooking the remaining crêpes in the same way, greasing the pan only when the crêpes start to stick.

As the crêpes are cooked, pile them one on top of the other to keep the first crêpes moist and warm. Crêpes can be made ahead, layered with waxed paper between each of them, and stored in a plastic bag. They can be kept in the refrigerator for up to 3 days, or they can be frozen.

Fillings & Frostings

(33) Butter-Cream Frosting
(CRÈME AU BEURRE)

Rich and smooth, butter cream is the favorite French frosting.

To make *1½ cups* (375 ml) frosting:

3 egg yolks
½ cup (100 g) sugar
¼ cup (60 ml) water
6 ounces (180 g) unsalted butter

To make *2 cups* (500 ml) frosting:

4 egg yolks
⅔ cup (135 g) sugar
⅓ cup (80 ml) water
½ pound (250 g) unsalted butter

In a bowl beat the egg yolks lightly until mixed. Heat the sugar with the water until dissolved, bring to a boil, and boil until the syrup reaches the soft-ball stage (239°F or 115°C on a candy thermometer). Gradually pour the hot sugar syrup onto the egg yolks, beating constantly, and continue beating until the mixture is cool and thick.

Cream the butter, then gradually beat it into the cool egg mixture. Beat in the flavoring.

Egg-yolk butter-cream frosting can be kept in the refrigerator for up to 1 week, or it can be frozen. Let it come to room temperature and beat thoroughly before using.

(34) Pastry Cream
(CRÈME PÂTISSIÈRE)

Pastry cream is the base for most sweet soufflés and a component of many tarts. It is also used as a filling for cakes and choux pastries (hence the name "cream puffs" for choux in English). A lighter filling can be made by combining equal quantities of pastry cream and Chantilly cream (**36**).

To make *1½ cups* (310 ml) pastry cream:

3 egg yolks
4 tablespoons (50 g) sugar
2 tablespoons (15 g) flour
1 cup (250 ml) milk, in all
pinch salt
1 vanilla bean OR ½ teaspoon vanilla extract—optional

To make *1¾ cups* (435 ml) pastry cream:

5 egg yolks
6 tablespoons (65 g) sugar
4 tablespoons (30 g) flour
1½ cups (375 ml) milk, in all
pinch salt
1 vanilla bean OR ¾ teaspoon vanilla extract—optional

To make *2¼ cups* (560 ml) pastry cream:

6 egg yolks

240

½ cup (100 g) sugar
5 tablespoons (45 g) flour
2 cups (500 ml) milk, in all
big pinch salt
1 vanilla bean OR 1 teaspoon vanilla extract—optional

Beat the egg yolks with the sugar until thick and light. Stir in the flour and enough milk to make a smooth paste. Scald the remaining milk with the salt. If using a vanilla bean, add it to the hot milk, cover, and leave to infuse 10–15 minutes. Remove the bean and wash it to use again. Reheat the milk to boiling.

Whisk the boiling milk into the yolk mixture, return to the pan, and whisk over gentle heat until boiling. (NOTE: Be sure the pastry cream is smooth before allowing it to boil.) If lumps form as the mixture thickens, take the pan from the heat and beat until smooth.

Cook the cream gently, whisking constantly, for 2 minutes or until it thins slightly, showing that the flour is completely cooked. If using vanilla extract, add it now. If the cream is too stiff, add a little milk. Take the cream from the heat, transfer it to a bowl, and rub a piece of butter over the surface, or sprinkle with powdered sugar to prevent a skin from forming. Cover only after it has cooled.

Pastry cream can be stored, tightly covered, in the refrigerator, a day or two.

(35) *Custard Sauce*
(CRÈME ANGLAISE)

Some cooks like to make custard sauce in a double boiler to ensure that it does not get too hot and curdle. It can be flavored with vanilla, lemon or orange rind, or liqueur, and can be served hot or cold.

To make *1¼ cups* (310 ml) custard sauce:

1 cup (250 ml) milk
1 vanilla bean OR ½ teaspoon vanilla extract—optional

3 egg yolks
2 tablespoons (25 g) sugar

To make 2¼ *cups* (560 ml) custard sauce:
2 cups (500 ml) milk
1 vanilla bean OR 1 teaspoon vanilla extract—optional
6 egg yolks
4 tablespoons (50 g) sugar

To make 3½ *cups* (875 ml) custard sauce:

3 cups (750 ml) milk
1 vanilla bean OR 1½ teaspoons vanilla extract—optional
9 egg yolks
6 tablespoons (80 g) sugar

Bring the milk with the vanilla bean almost to a boil and leave in a warm place to infuse 10–15 minutes. Remove the bean and wash it to use again. Beat the egg yolks with the sugar until thick and light. Reheat the milk to boiling. Whisk half the hot milk into the yolks and whisk this mixture back into the remaining milk. Heat gently, stirring constantly with a wooden spoon, until the custard thickens slightly; if you draw a finger across the back of the spoon, it should leave a clear trail. (NOTE: Do not overcook or boil, or it will curdle.)

Take the sauce from the heat at once and strain it into a bowl. If using vanilla extract, add it now. Stir often as the hot sauce cools. If serving cold, let cool completely, cover tightly, and chill. The sauce can be kept up to 2 days in the refrigerator.

(36) *Chantilly Cream*
(CRÈME CHANTILLY)

This is the easiest, and for many desserts the best, topping. Chantilly cream is also folded into other toppings and fillings to lighten them. Of course, this is the whipped cream of our childhood, which many of us probably first encountered on strawberry shortcake.

1 cup (250 ml) heavy cream
1 tablespoon (12 g) sugar
½ teaspoon vanilla extract

Makes about 2 cups (500 ml) cream.

Chill the cream, bowl, and whisk before whipping. Beat the cream until it starts to thicken. Add the sugar and vanilla and continue beating until the cream sticks to the whisk. Be careful not to overbeat, or the cream will turn to butter.

Chantilly cream can be kept 1–2 hours in the refrigerator without separating. Whisk it before using.

(37) *Sugar Syrup for Moistening Cakes*
(SIROP À GÂTEAU)

French cakes tend to be dry, so the layers are often moistened with syrup before they are assembled.

1 cup (200 g) sugar
1 cup (250 ml) water
1 tablespoon, or to taste, kirsch, Grand Marnier, or other liqueur
    —optional

Makes 1 cup (250 ml) syrup.

Heat the sugar with the water over low heat until dissolved, then boil 2–3 minutes or until the syrup is clear. Stir in flavoring. The sugar syrup can be kept up to 2 months in the refrigerator.

(38) *Apricot Glaze*
(NAPPAGE)

Used to glaze fruit tarts and pastries.

> 1 cup (300 g) apricot preserves
> ¼ cup (50 g) sugar

Makes 1 cup (350 ml) glaze.

Strain the preserves into a pan and stir in the sugar. Bring to a boil and cook, stirring, for 3 minutes or until the sugar is completely dissolved. The glaze can be kept, covered, in the refrigerator for several months. Reheat before using.

(39) *Praline*
(PRALINE)

Praline is used to flavor butter cream, pastry cream, meringues, and a variety of desserts.

To make ⅔ *cup* (200 g) praline:

> ⅔ cup (100 g) whole unblanched almonds (that is, with their skins)
> ½ cup (100 g) sugar

To make *1 cup* (300 g) praline:

1 cup (150 g) whole unblanched almonds
¾ cup (150 g) sugar

To make *1⅓ cups* (400 g) praline:

1⅓ cups (200 g) whole unblanched almonds
1 cup (200 g) sugar

Combine the almonds and sugar in a heavy-bottomed pan. Stir over low heat until the sugar melts. Continue cooking slowly until the sugar turns a golden brown and the almonds literally pop, showing they are toasted. Pour the mixture onto an oiled marble slab or baking sheet. Leave until cool and crisp. Grind to a powder, a little at a time, in a blender, food processor, rotary cheese grater, or in a mortar with a pestle. The praline can be kept for several weeks in an airtight container.

(40) Swiss Meringue
(MERINGUE SUISSE)

Swiss meringue is used for toppings and sometimes for meringue cases and cakes.

    4 egg whites
    1¼ cups (250 g) sugar
    1 teaspoon vanilla extract—optional

Makes about 2½ cups (625 ml) meringue.
    Beat the egg whites until stiff, if possible in a copper bowl. Add 4 teaspoons of the sugar and continue beating for another minute or until the egg whites are glossy. Fold in the remaining sugar a few tablespoons at a time. Fold in the vanilla with the last spoonful of

sugar. (NOTE: Do not overmix, or the mixture will become liquid as the sugar dissolves.)

Swiss meringue can be kept, covered with a damp cloth, in the refrigerator, but after an hour it will start to separate.

(41) How to Make Crème Fraîche

This is not strictly speaking a basic recipe in French cuisine, since in France most cream in the markets is already made into the renowned, lightly fermented crème fraîche. But, in the United States, you must make your own, which is not difficult, but is important especially for sauces (see p. 32).

2 cups (500 ml) heavy cream
1 cup (250 ml) buttermilk, sour cream, or yogurt

Makes 3 cups (750 ml) crème fraîche.

In a saucepan stir together the heavy cream and buttermilk, sour cream, or yogurt. Heat gently until the mixture is just body temperature. Pour into a container and partially cover. Leave at room temperature 6–8 hours or overnight, or until thickened and slightly acid in taste. (NOTE: On a hot day, the cream may thicken faster; on a cold day, it will take longer.) Stir the cream, cover, and refrigerate.

Crème fraîche can be kept up to 1 week in the refrigerator. The longer it stands, the thicker and more pronounced in flavor it will become.

When making a *new* batch of crème fraîche, 1 cup (250 ml) of crème fraîche that you have already made can be used instead of the buttermilk, sour cream, or yogurt.

NOTE: Crème fraîche is better made with buttermilk than with sour cream. It is least good made with yogurt, but keeps the longest. Sour cream-based crème fraîche has the shortest keeping time.

Menu Planning Index

PASTRIES AND SWEETS

Recipe Index